TO BE
OR
TO BECOME

The Emzine Dialogue

MARC VAN DER ERVE

THE EMZINE DIALOGUE

Philosophical Dialogue

For information about the author, consult the following website:
www.marcvandererve.org

To share your critique, consult the following website:
www.emzine.net

To buy this book in another form, consult the following website:
www.tobeortobecome.com

ISBN:
Digital version: 978-0-620-49858-6
Hardcopy: 978-0-620-49857-9

Cover photo:
Upper dome of the Cathedral of Sienna taken by the author.

TO BE
OR
TO BECOME

To Karen Evelien

Content

Introduction

At the beginning of the third millennium in what is often called the Common Era, an exceptional dialogue unfolded. The exchange produced a novel window onto Nature that allows us to predict and enhance the emergence of our world beyond what we thought possible at the time. Unveiling the emergent nature of Nature and not dreamed up to take advantage of the desire of man to explore his origin, this window meets the rigorous standards upheld by the world of science.

I had the privilege of participating in this dialogue on a journey that took us from one finding to another until reaching enlightenment by the identification of what we called the "Emzine." A new acronym, *Emzine* stands for *Existential Manifold Zine*. The *Existential Manifold* refers to all that we observe. *Zine* stems from magazine. *Emzine* is the hidden *zine* where Nature "writes" the realities that we observe. The story in this book revolves around the question of what this writing is about. What (or who) "writes" all that we observe, and what can and should we do with this knowledge?

The views of reality at the heart of claims by scientists, philosophers, and religious leaders at the time left too many questions unanswered. The idea of *Emzine* offers a lucid alternative without the need to veer off into exotic realms of explanation, such as quantum mechanics, nonetheless valid in these domains. Not requiring new information about our world but inspired by a novel reading of existing data, the idea of *Emzine* represents a true Copernican revolution.

In the future, children will probably learn about *Emzine*, the hidden side of reality, even before they learn about the birds and the bees. Then again, whereas the idea of *Emzine* may reach society, the tale of its emergence may not. This is why I pieced together precious fragments of history into a story about the unveiling of the *path of Emzine*. Of course, the account in this book is what I noted. Any omissions are due to the limits of my recollection.

Eve

Prologue

M was patiently waiting backstage for the announcer to finish his introduction speech.

Strangely enough, many people in the audience did not know what M stood for. The name or qualification of M surfaced in the past as acknowledgement of a phenomenon that was part man part insight, an insight that had changed the prospects for human society. M himself did not bother, 'My name should not be in the way of the message.'

People from nearly every corner of the earth had come to Cape Town for an assembly that M would address as keynote speaker. An audience of more than a thousand people had flocked through the four-story high hallway of the city's international conference center.

More than a decade had gone by after the second global economic crisis in a century had vaporized trillions of dollars. Now, under the successor of President Jacob Zuma, South Africa had acquired a new sense of identity that functioned as a platform for a new cycle of growth.

The remarkable fit of the nation's leader had been attributed to the advice of M during the preselection of presidential candidates. Other than that his insight might have guided the process, he denied any such direct influence. It was no secret though that these two personalities knew each other.

As the announcer continued with his opening words, M noticed the restlessness of the audience. In the solitude of his backstage position, he dwelled on the true meaning of the occasion and on his lecture for this gathering, which was organized to celebrate the beginning of an era.

With a tingle of sadness, he realized that, only a decade ago, today's meeting would have been unthinkable.

His tiring one-track life dawned on him, a life that had slowly and doggedly edged forward in the face of academic and public denial, a life of holding back until holding back was no longer an option.

When his persistence finally brought him to the surreal shores of success, he saw to his surprise that society did not surrender but opened up. Apparently, the time was ripe.

He stared off into the distance and thought to himself, 'Even events early in life contributed to a growing awareness of a world that can be traced back to the conduct of things, anything from people and particles to electromagnetic fields.'

The fifth born in a family of seven and too young to participate in the world of his kin, he had become an observer and wonderer.

As a three-year-old with fair hair that had hardly been cut, he had vanished from his mother's sight, leaving her in a state of panic. She feared that he might have drowned in the public pond across the street. She could not believe the officer who called her with the news that his colleagues had found an infant on a train to a city nearby.

At the age of ten, when the world entered the space age, his view of the world broadened with each rocket launch.

Three years later, he first questioned his mother about the religious rituals upheld by his father. During the pre-Easter fasting that year, he complained, 'Other than that refraining from eating doesn't appear to change us, such rituals distract us from our search for the true motive of human conduct,' a comment that his mother seemed to accept in silence.

The differences between his views and those of his father became more articulated when he flourished as a student of physics. However, the sincerity of his father's dependence on religion as a code of morality and permanence not only kept their exchanges civilized but also prevented M from denying his father's or anybody's faith.

'Religion played an unmistakable role in the emergence of today's society,' is what he maintained throughout his life.

'Then again,' he usually added, 'the answer to the fallible premises of religions is not in the creation of another religion. We should rather find the means to rise above religion.'

The thought occurred to him that he had decided to reiterate this in his speech today. The astonishing insight into the true nature of Nature, that he had the privilege of unveiling many years ago, had put matters of science and religion in a new perspective.

He looked forward to meeting the people who had once helped him explore the explanation of a phenomenon that produces and explains human existence and much more than that.

Unexpectedly, someone entered the backstage area. Recovering from his self-imposed trance, it took M only an instant to bring back this face from the past.

'Oh, hi! How are you?'

'I am fine!'

Just then, the announcer finished his introduction. It was M's turn to get on stage.

One stride before stepping into the limelight, M stopped and looked back with a puzzled expression on his face, his posture frozen for an instant. Then, he slowly turned around, searched for his speech notes and headed for the speaker's stand in a statesmanlike fashion.

When he was halfway, the unthinkable happened. Without any warning, all lights were switched off, leaving total darkness and an audience too baffled to react.

As M was knocked down, his time was brutally cut short. The last thing his ears registered was a muffled explosion but that realization failed to reach him. His mind was blank.

The Divine Domain

His gaze moved beyond her and the hidden mountain terrace, his eyes passively absorbing the stunning red sky of the sunset unfolding over Table Mountain some 40 miles away.

'I unveiled an astonishing world of insight, a world that explains the reality that we observe and experience. I wonder why this world has not been identified before. It seems *so* obvious, in hindsight!'

She looked at him, empathizing.

'This reminds me of Plato,' he added.

'What does an ancient Greek philosopher have to do with this?'

'Have you heard of Plato's Cave Allegory?'

'Frankly, I haven't!'

'It's a parable in which Plato follows his usual pattern by letting his beloved teacher, Socrates, do the story'

'Tell me!'

'Socrates explores the worldview of prisoners that have been chained to the walls inside a cave since their childhood. Facing the back of the cave and unable to see the cave's entrance, these prisoners have no idea of the real world outside. When it comes to the world of insight that I identified, people often resemble these prisoners.'

'I sense where you are heading but the point you want to make is not yet exactly clear to me!'

'Well, the movement of guards walking around a large fire in front of the cave's mouth produced shimmering light and echo on the walls in the back of the cave. The prisoners, who could do nothing but watch this, adopted the theatre of moving shadows and sounds as their main source of explanation. In time, these faint features of echo and light inspired the invention of ingenious theories about how the world outside the cave might function.

'My point is that the theories of these prisoners are not unlike the theories that people use to explain our world today.'

He hesitated briefly as if he was not certain whether to continue. Yet, she gestured him to go on.

'Plato's parable involves a prisoner who manages to escape. Before being recaptured and returned to the cave, the escapee experienced the world outside for real.

'As you can imagine, whenever the prisoners theorized about the world outside, the escapee would challenge their analyses.'

"Look, I have seen the real world outside," 'he would say.' "It really is different from what you say it is!"

'Not prepared to dismiss the theories that had nourished their sense of identity for years, the prisoners bullied the runaway. Had they not been chained to the cave's walls, they would have even killed him! In the end, being kept in check by their chains, the prisoners chose to ignore the outsider.'

'I see what you mean. I bet you feel like an outsider, right?'

'In a sense, I do. I had no choice! To see the real world outside, I had to become an escapee, as it were.

'Now that I think about it, while the theories of the prisoners served as *anchors of interpretation*, their chains served as *moral anchors*.'

'Why?'

'Because they prevented the prisoners from killing the escapee!

'Curiously, some of the moral anchors today feel like chains as well.'

'Hmm, our moral anchors prevent us from reaching and interpreting the real world outside the cave! If this is true, so much more is at stake when it comes to the world that you unveiled. What in the world outside the cave will replace the traditional anchors of morality? This bodes trouble for the usual sources of morality, such as religion, I figure!'

'Anyway, unveiling is what I did. I didn't invent anything. I simply raised the cloth that conceals the way that Nature follows to produce the realities that we observe.'

She pointed to the surroundings of the mountain terrace at the heart of what is called Hidden Valley and laughed.

'Finding this place off the R44 somewhere between Somerset West and Stellenbosch is like finding the world that you are talking about!'

'That's right! Furthermore, when you follow the narrow path that leads to this exceptional location and restaurant, you'll see your destiny only at the very last moment, just before you arrive. The question is how do you encourage people or prisoners, for that matter, to take this path and persevere. This is the challenge that I am facing, as escapee.'

'When it comes to Hidden Valley, people are encouraged by the exquisite cuisine and dazzling view from here. People may not have been attracted to the world of insight that you unveiled because it fails to offer such benefits! Isn't that why people have been missing your point?'

'I don't think so! The world of insight that I am referring to offers remarkable benefits. For one, our world would become so much more predictable. Imagine an ability to see the world unfolding ahead of us, an ability that would allow us to instill measures today that will improve its functioning tomorrow. Such an ability would also allow us to identify the right type of leadership needed at the various levels of society.

'If you'd understand the process that Nature follows to arrive at the realities that we observe you might even improve on Nature itself and achieve realities that seem impossible now.

'No, in my view, it is not a lack of benefits that makes people waver.

'There must be another reason.

'For example, the world of insight that I unveiled might simply be too remote from established theories. Mind you, for thousands of years, people have been judging the world from within their cave, so to speak.'

'Wait a minute! You are saying that *they* are cave prisoners but what prevents them from claiming that *you* are a cave prisoner with a theory that, they might say, is less refined than theirs?'

'The world that I unveiled lies outside any cave, yet describes what takes place inside each cave.'

'You mean, it's a kind of theory of everything?'

'I suppose you could say that, but it is a theory of everything that differs from those that have been proposed so far.'

'I really don't get that!'

'Traditional theories of everything are produced by physicists, such as Albert Einstein. Typically, these theories are centered on the subatomic domain, where energy and matter are interchangeable. They are called theories of everything because most of what we observe in our world involves energy and matter in some form or another.'

'So, what is wrong with these theories of everything?'

'Nothing wrong with these theories, that is, if indeed experiments confirm what these theories predict. When they do, they are only valid in a specific domain. These theories can rarely be used straightforwardly in any other branch of science or in any other cave, if you like.'

'Can you illustrate this with an example?'

'Several attempts have been made to explain behavioral situations in organizations by relating them to subatomic or quantum-mechanical theories. However, these theories cannot sensibly be used to describe what goes on there. Different circumstances, rules and actors apply in much the same way as different circumstances, rules and actors apply in electromechanical and biological systems.

'To be frank, I am highly skeptical of some of these over-creative and sometimes plainly misleading attempts by popular thinkers who try to explain day-to-day situations simply by swapping laws between distinct and even far-out domains of science.

'However strong the symbolic value of these attempts, they do not get us any further in a practical sense.'

'Hmm, that adds up, I must admit.'

'Of course, the worldview that I unveiled comes with rules of its own. Yet, it stands out because it explains the realities in our world no matter what the circumstances or actors!

'I mean, it explains matters that are observed *across* the sciences or across the different caves, so to speak. It doesn't involve a new cave but *a new window* onto the world outside the cave.

'Interestingly, the view through this window adds to current theories rather than replaces them.'

'What you are telling me sounds very ambitious, I must say.

'It may be too much to expect from people that they persevere on this path of inquiry. After all, matters of reality have been fiercely debated for thousands of years by philosophers, scientists and leaders of thought from all walks of life.'

'It is interesting that you bring up this point.

'The worldview that I unveiled gives oxygen to the ideas of important philosophers. However, it is a bit too early to ask these philosophers to reconcile the worldview that I unveiled.'

She looked puzzled when he referred to philosophers from the past as if they were still around but she left it at that.

'The problem is that, so far, all of us have been studying our world as historians.'

'Historians?' she asked.

'Yes, historians!'

'Please, explain!'

'The breakthrough and survival of modern humans or *Homo sapiens sapiens*, which stands for *wise, wise man* by the way, didn't just hinge on their superior communication skills nor on their ability to remember and recognize events, nor on their capacity to craft tools. Neanderthals were as good at it. As the caves in the Cro-Magnon region of France and those in South Africa and elsewhere overwhelmingly show, modern humans distinguished themselves by their ability to trust abstractions of the events that they experienced to the walls of their cave shelters, as drawings!'

'Most interesting!'

'Through these abstractions, modern humans not only made the interpretations of their world more accessible. They also created a common framework of reference that enabled them to align the interpretations of their world and grow the vocabulary needed to exchange their experiences as well as the sentiments that these enticed. Most importantly, these abstractions helped accelerate the transmission of experiences that had been shown to lead to success.'

'I never looked at it like that!'

'The transmission of experiences determined how modern humans describe and analyze their world. Ultimately, in the pursuit of evermore-rapid success, they added time to event descriptions—for example, the time it takes to accomplish goals. This way, events that produced results faster could be identified.

'This is where the crucial idea of *time* comes in.'

'I see!'

'Time plays a role in the sequence and timing of our actions. Both learning from and improving on the past involve time. As a result, measures of time are now at the center of almost every branch of trade and science.'

'Can you expand on this, please?'

'Well, today, you'd hardly ever log an event by noting the spatial conditions only. Time is nearly always part of event analyses. For example, whereas historians analyze diaries of past events, management assistants analyze diaries of future events. Even physicists explain how one event produces another. Although they use mathematical equations in the process, the spirit of what they do resembles the approach of historians.'

'So, where does all this lead?'

'This all has one crucial consequence.

'The very skills that explain our success as a species prevent us now from improving the way we observe and interpret our world. Most if not all humans, historians and physicists included, appear to be confined to an overarching cave where the features of echo and light on the walls get meaning through time intervals. In our world today, we create meaning through time.'

'I don't see why this is catastrophic!'

'No, it isn't, that is, until we run into a wall.'

'Have we done so?'

'Well, yes, we have! What's worse, we have done so in various ways.'

'Which wall?'

'When the length of a time interval gets shorter and shorter until it is just about nil, a virtual wall appears that blocks our view and spoils our analyses. When that happens, we lose the thing that helps us explain the events in our world and their emergence.'

'Can you give me some practical examples because I have difficulty picturing this wall?'

'Okay, I'll tackle the difficult examples first.'

'Sure!'

'In the world of physics, some mathematical models are referred to as singularities because they predict an infinite rate of change or an infinite other result when the time interval in these models reduces to nil.

'According to one such model, the rate of the expansion of the early universe is infinite at the beginning of time when the time interval is nil. Of course, an infinite rate of expansion would produce an exceptionally big bang. This is how the Big Bang theory about the birth of the universe emerged. Physicists now assume that something is missing from these models. On the whole, in a world where we create meaning through time, we are likely to run into a pointless wall of extremes when a time interval reduces to nil.'

'This is all very complicated but I see your point.'

'At subatomic levels, quantum physics describes the appearance of phenomena, such as fundamental particles. Curiously, an externally clocked time that tracks the emergence of these phenomena is missing from these models of description. Instead, these models calculate the probability of phenomena appearing. Both physicists and philosophers refer to this issue as the lack of emergent time. [1] This issue has, so far, not been resolved. Again, the time intervals at these levels are very short and approaching zero because very short distances are travelled at exceptionally high speeds. The virtual wall that we run into here forces us to surrender to the idea that our world is ruled by chance.'

'I see! I hope your next example is closer to home.'

'My next and most important example is!'

---

[1] *The Arguments of Time*, Oxford University Press, 2006

'Why will this be your most important example?'

'For two reasons really! First, it directly concerns us, people. Second, it is an unavoidable consequence of the way society develops.'

'Let's go for it!'

'The introduction of the Internet and the continuing efforts to install faster and denser communication networks produces a society where we lose perspective of sequence. Remember that I said that the sequence of events helps us establish the timing of our actions?

'In a densely networked society, events may unfold so rapidly that they appear to unfold at the same time. As a result, we have difficulty determining the timing of our actions. Instinctively, we understand that the emergence of one event will somehow trigger the emergence of other events. However, when the time intervals between events become ever shorter, our logic of sequential or historical interpretation serves us no longer. The chaos of near simultaneously rising events shapes the virtual wall that we run into here!'

'Information-technology firms no doubt react to the uncertainty that this brings by offering more comprehensive systems!'

'That's right! However, these systems do not fundamentally change anything. They only make it possible to zoom in on corporate events and show the sequence of events again.

'Unfortunately, at the same time, they encourage leaders to continue to evaluate their companies as historians. As a result, leaders fail to pick the fruits of *simultaneity*.'

She ignored what he had just said, yet registered it subconsciously.

'They speak of turning organizations into "dexterous organizations." Do you know what they mean by that?'

'That term pops up regularly lately. Dexterity involves more agile or acute organizations that are supposed to be able to innovate their way out of these so-called complexity traps.'

'Hmm...'

'You can say that! The notion of dexterity temporarily extends the road of historical analyses and only postpones the moment when we run into a wall.

'Let's face it, on the whole, the virtual wall that blocks our view and spoils our analyses is shaped by extremes, chance and the near-simultaneous and chaotic rise of events on all scales.'

'So, where do we go from here?'

'Beyond, the wall.'

'You mean outside the cave?'

'Yes, because that's where the realities that we observe in the back of the cave are produced.'

'If the overarching cave in your example represents the world in which we live then whose world is the world outside the cave? The divine?'

'The clue is in the wall that blocks our view.'

'I don't get it.'

'As my examples illustrate, the chaos of simultaneously emerging events that disrupts our serial logic of interpretation is evidence of the domain where Nature produces new realities.

'So, the world outside the cave in Plato's Cave Allegory might not be a separate physical world but a domain where simultaneity rather than time intervals determine things.

'In other words, the world that we observe in the back of the cave is ruled by *time intervals* and the world outside the cave by *simultaneity*, simultaneity meaning events separated by time*less* intervals or time intervals that equal nil.'

'I see! So the world inside and outside the cave are effectively part of our world but each functions in another domain of time!'

'Yes, you might say that.'

'This is truly thought-provoking.'

'Not really! The idea is about 4500 years old.'

'That's about 2000 years before Plato lived!'

'I was as surprised as you are when I discovered this in one of the books of the Egyptologist, Jan Assmann.[2]

'I contacted professor Assmann and he was kind enough to send me an email with the script of a speech in which he details his findings.'

---

[2] *Moses The Egyptian*, Harvard University Press, 1998

'Enlighten me!'

'The ancient Pyramid texts refer to two domains of time: "a time of reality" and "a time that goes by" or "Time Great" and "Time Small."

'According to the ancient Egyptians, *Time Great* is the time used in the divine world. They identified it as "a time of preexistence and post-existence," a time that is "not linear but of cycles, endless in the cosmic life."

'The ancient Egyptians believed that the King's tomb functioned as a gate, which would give access to the world of the divine and to *Time Great*.'

'Am I correct to assume, therefore, that the King's tomb is the gate to the world outside the cave in Plato's Cave Allegory?'

'I think so because, according to the ancient Egyptians, *Time Great* is the divine domain of time "where new realities emerge."'

'Consequently, *Time Small* must be the domain of time intervals that we observe in the back of the cave.'

'Absolutely! The ancient Egyptians refer to *Time Small* as a time that is like "a dream that passes," a time that "governs on Earth" or in our cave, so to speak.'

'Those are the features of time as interval, all right!'

'I think, it's time to wrap up. Don't you agree?'

'I guess, you are right. This has been something; amazing, yet real at the same time!'

He laughed and called a waiter.

'Would you like a dessert?'

'No, thanks, just a coffee. Make it an espresso! I need it to return from Plato's cave to our world.'

'Oh, this was just a beginning. If you'd like, we'll explore this further. You really helped me get to the core of my ideas by peeling the onion, as it were.'

'I'd love to!'

Reality's Amazing Parallel

The scenery along the R44 between Somerset West and Stellenbosch always pleased him. The rolling landscape checkered with wineries and surrounded by bare mountains that seemed to have been imported straight from Mars never failed to give him a deep sense of gratitude— gratitude for the privilege of being able to spend part of his life here.

He turned right into the Village Road or Dorp Straat and parked his car near the little white church in the center of Stellenbosch. Every Sunday, this charming place of worship drew droves of students, all neatly dressed and holding their Bibles.

His meeting place, a street café called Java, was two blocks away. At the heart of the old city, Java was the favorite meeting place for students, scholars and, of course, tourists. The café's street terrace was usually crowded. Yet it nearly always left room for other guests.

When he arrived he had to study the terrace scene for a moment, then soon discovered her drinking a cappuccino. He walked over to her table.

'Hi, have you been waiting long?'

'No, not at all! They have only just served my cappuccino. Would you like one too?'

'Just a coffee will be fine.

'Have you recovered from our conversation?'

'I did! We sure reached great philosophical depths!'

'I'd like to explore more practical examples this stretch, Eve.'

'Why are you calling me Eve?'

'It is a symbolic name that expresses the important role you play.'

'Why Eve? And who are you?'

'Not Adam if that's what you think. I use Eve as a short form for *eve*ryone. No pun intended!

'Take my word, your help in waking up humanity from what the ancient Egyptians called "a dream that passes" will make you the mother of a new understanding.'

'I see,' she said coolly. 'Then, who are you?'

'Call me M.'

'What does *that* stand for?'

'It's symbolic too. At the center of the alphabet, M is the thirteenth letter. More notably, the letter M is balanced in the middle and has two feet on the ground.

'What I am really trying to say is that, when it comes to findings that improve the prospects of human kind, findings rather than names are important.'

'Come on! Didn't you choose the letter M because it suggests you are a *messenger* or a *medium* or... a *messiah*?'

'Oh no! Whose messenger *would* I be? I am nobody's messenger.

'I am not a medium either, a medium of what, by the way?

'Above all, I am neither messiah nor liberator. The findings that I refer to did not rise to the surface to counter a tyranny of some kind nor do they represent a prophecy or scripture coming true. As I'll explain later on, they emerged by harmony rather than conflict.'

'Then, who *are* you?'

'As I said yesterday, I am an escapee who returned to the cave that we all share. However ambitious it may sound, I bring a view of how the world that we observe in the back of the cave really emerges. You might say that I opened a window onto the world outside the cave, a window that is bound to change what we see and believe.'

'Did history also produce other escapees?'

'It did! For example, in the Renaissance, when Western society woke up from its medieval nap, Copernicus and Galileo became escapees.'

'Tell me!'

'At the time of Copernicus, the consensus was that the Earth was at rest in the center of the universe. Nearly two thousand years ago, Ptolemy, a Roman citizen of Egypt, introduced this view. Ptolemy also invented a related mathematical model of the universe. This model, which involved a set of nested spheres, made it possible to calculate the positions of the Sun, Moon and planets quite accurately.'

'So, when does Copernicus come into the story?'

'Fourteen hundred years after Ptolemy introduced his view of the universe, Copernicus, a Polish astronomer, evaluated Ptolemy's theory and concluded that the paths of celestial bodies could be explained much more simply if the Earth rotated around the Sun. This way he disproved the common perception that the Earth was at the center of the universe, a perception that had ruled the thinking of societal leaders for centuries.

'Copernicus did not know more than Ptolemy had known, neither did he have better instruments. He just looked at the problem differently.

'As you can imagine, the views of Copernicus produced shock waves when societal leaders became aware of his findings.'

'Is this when Galileo made his entrance?'

'That's right! Galileo, an astronomer and physicist from Tuscany, made history when he openly underpinned the findings of Copernicus based on observations of planetary paths that were made possible by improvements to his telescope.'

'Is that so?'

'Galileo's proof of the world outside the cave, as it were, made it impossible to dismiss the findings of Copernicus as theory. Facing a path of fundamental change, clerical leaders at the time reacted as can often be expected. They denied Galileo's findings and put him under house arrest hoping to preserve a worldview that they had conveniently adhered to since the early days of Christianity.'

'This bodes trouble for you as escapee.'

'I realize that only too well.

'Anyway, escapees are not just mind-shifters. They are people who saw the world outside the cave, where reality emerges.'

'This means you cannot be an escapee if you are chained to the walls in the back of the cave.'

'Indeed!'

'So, if I could manage to see the world outside the cave, I would be an escapee too!'

'That's right. Everyone can become an escapee.

'However, as you suggested yesterday, because traditional chains of morality no longer secure escapees, they need to embrace a new source of morality.'

'I'd be curious to know more about this source.'

'You will in time!'

'So, for the sake of transmission clarity in future eras, I hope it's all right if I call you Eve.'

She nodded approvingly.

'Shall we recap our chat yesterday?'

Eve did not respond. She appeared to have become aware of her environment and looked anxiously at the people sitting at a table next to them.

'What's wrong?'

'I saw this man sitting close to us yesterday.'

'I see!'

An older man with thick silver hair and a clean-cut silver beard looked in their direction. A woman sat next to him. They sat comfortably with the terrace crowd. The man noticed Eve's unease and smiled at her.

'Yesterday, I was sitting at a table next to you. By chance, we meet again. It's a true privilege!'

Eve's nod was barely noticeable.

'It is not my intention to intrude but we couldn't prevent hearing fragments of your most interesting exchange on a topic that is close to my heart. I reckon, you're about to continue your dialogue!'

'Indeed, we were just about to,' M answered.

'Allow me to introduce myself. I am Umberto and this is my wife, Phil. We are from Europe. I am a manufacturing engineer and academic.

Since my retirement, I have become increasingly interested in matters that improve our grasp of both Nature and society.

'I don't want to impose myself nor disturb the flow of your chat but we'd be honored to be part of the audience.'

'Please, feel free to listen in and participate, if you'd like!'

M continued as if nothing had happened, 'Where were we?'

With renewed vigor, Eve summarized her recollection of their chat the day before.

'In Plato's Cave Allegory, the world observed in the back of the cave is a reflection of the world outside the cave where reality truly emerges. Whereas time intervals give meaning to the echo and images on the walls in the back of the cave, simultaneity rules in the world outside the cave.

'In Plato's Cave Allegory, the world outside the cave is detached from the world observed in the back of the cave. However, in reality these two worlds might not be separated physically. Both may be part of the world that we live in.'

'If I may,' Umberto interjected, 'the challenge that you seem to be facing is how you'd identify the world that is ruled by simultaneity.'

'I suppose, you should try to focus on simultaneous matters because they mark the world outside the cave where reality emerges. However, off the cuff, I wouldn't know how to do that.'

'If I may, I still have a hard time dealing with the relation between time interval or time and simultaneity!' Phil said.

Umberto's body language signaled that Phil had raised a point worthy of note.

'It's great that you bring this up, Phil! We shouldn't rush into a search for simultaneous matters without properly understanding this relation.'

'So, the issue is time! What is time, *really*?' Umberto concluded.

'A time interval or, simply, time is a human invention,' M said.

For a moment, Eve looked concerned when she heard M make this claim. Umberto did not even blink.

'Let me try to explain.

'As we discussed yesterday, time helps humans compare different events. For example, travelers might decide to travel one or the other route based on the number of days that each route would take.

'However, what does it mean to measure time in days, such as the days needed to travel from say Europe to China?'

Eve and Phil shrugged.

'When you measure time in days, you essentially count the Earth's rotations from the moment you leave until the moment you arrive. After all, each Earth rotation represents one day, right?'

'Of course!' Eve said.

'In other words, time is a translation of the motion of the journey into the spinning motion of the Earth because the motion of the journey is expressed in Earth rotations or days. So time is relative.'

'Relative? What do you mean by that?' Eve asked.

'Well, time emerges only after relating simultaneous events of which one event involves repeated movements, such as the rotation of the Earth. Without such an event to relate to, time fails to transpire.'

'Will you please explain this again?' Phil asked.

'Sure! Time involves counting the repeated movements of another event that unfolds at the same time. In other words, time doesn't stand on itself. Its emergence depends on a reference event.'

'I see what you mean,' Eve said, 'but, doesn't this also apply if you use a clock to measure time?'

'The principle remains the same. For example, analogue clocks are built in such a way that the big hand steadily spins twenty-four times each Earth rotation. Each spin of the clock's big hand has historically been defined as one hour. So, when you use a clock to measure time, you essentially translate the motion of an event into the motion of the clock's big hand, the number of its rotations revealing the duration of the event in hours.'

Eve stared into the distance pensively. 'Am I right to assume that history could also have produced a clock whereby the big hand spins twenty times each Earth rotation?'

'Absolutely!'

'So, how would the prisoners in Plato's cave have measured time, if they did at all?' Phil asked.

She looked at Umberto who seemed eager to restate her question.

'This involves two questions, really! How would the cave prisoners have measured time and, second, why would they?'

'Starting with your first question: in the back of the cave, the prisoners could not see the recurrence of night and day. So they were forced to look for other events that involved repetitive movement. For example, the reappearance of a guard bringing their daily food ration would serve as a hand of their imaginary cave clock. So would the echo of the regular change of the guard outside. These repeated events helped the prisoners reestablish a sense of time that involved counting meals and changes of guard rather than days and hours.

'The prisoners were keen to reestablish their notion of time not just because it provided them with a sense of past but, particularly, because it allowed them to anticipate the future.'

Eve looked mildly confused.

'The capacity to make projections of what the future might bring and how to go about that future, however constrained, is at the heart of our inner sense of identity. If the cave prisoners had failed to regain their grasp of time, their sense of being would have diminished even to an extent that would impair their physical and mental health. This is in line with the known effects of solitary confinement, by the way!'

The idea of time both as abstract matter and as phenomenon that affects human wellbeing visibly surprised M's audience.

'If you'd allow me, I'll wrap up our understanding of time.'

'Time emerges from a relation between two events: that is, an event of which you'd like to measure the duration and a reference event that is recurrent. Because the measurement of time involves the translation of the motion of one event into the motion of another, recurrent event, time emerges from *motion*. This may seem trivial at this point but I'll explain later on why this is *so* important.'

'What makes time a human invention again?' Phil asked.

'It's choice: that is, the presumed freedom of selecting a reference event. Remember how the prisoners identified their recurrent events?'

'So far, we have not yet touched upon the most important feature at the heart of time.'

They all looked at M.

'Time will arise from the relation between two events only if these events unfold at the same time. So the measurement of time depends on simultaneity. In other words, we are free to choose both the event and the recurrent event as long as they are simultaneous.'

'What you are telling me is that the measurement of time itself engages simultaneity,' Eve said. 'Then, how, on Earth, do you identify the world, where simultaneity rules, if time itself and, thus, the world of time intervals depends on it? This essentially is the question that we started off with!'

'Because this time around, we are ready to answer it!'

Clearly humored by the interaction, Umberto watched Eve sigh with relief.

'Let's first have another coffee or would you rather have something else?' M asked.

It was then that he noticed one of the student waitresses standing nearby. Her terrace section was not yet filled to capacity and she had apparently followed the discussion from a distance because she was already on her way.

'I usually don't eavesdrop on the discussions of customers but this sure was intriguing, if I may say so.

'No problem!'

'You see, I am in the third year of my bachelor's in theology and philosophy is of one of my subjects.'

She left it at that and took their order.

When the waitress had served up, M picked up the thread of the discussion again.

'We are now ready to make a clear-cut distinction between the world of time intervals and the world of simultaneity.'

'I am curious, to say the least,' Eve said.

M laughed.

'To establish the duration of an event, we create artificial order by bringing together two not necessarily related events that happen to unfold simultaneously. This is what the world of time intervals is about. It's about a *deliberate* form of organization or order that we establish to arrive at a measure of time.'

'You mean, just like the cave prisoners derived their own order of things based on the events observed in the back of the cave?' Eve asked.

'That's right!

'In contrast, the world of simultaneity outside the cave concerns *spontaneously* or *naturally* emerging forms of organization or order.'

'You mean arising by itself or autonomously?' Eve asked.

'Indeed!'

'What do you mean by organization, again?' Eve asked.

'Organization involves orderly or repeated events that take place at the same time, events that may involve various actors.'

'What do you mean by actor? A movie actor?' Phil asked.

'Not really! I mean anyone or anything that plays a role in some form of organization.'

'Anything or anyone?'

'Well, events might involve people, objects, molecules, atoms and so on and any one of these might fulfill one or more roles in some form of organization or in some form of order.'

This struck a chord with Umberto.

'This is interesting! Do you mean to say that a form of organization might involve both human and non-human actors?'

'That's exactly what I mean to say!'

'So, the world of simultaneity that we are searching for concerns spontaneously emerging forms of organization that involve actors no matter who or what they are!' Umberto concluded.

'That's correct!'

'To pierce the world of simultaneity I reckon we should explore examples of spontaneously emerging forms of organization,' Eve said.

'That's what I'd like to suggest we do now.'

'Do you know the name, Erwin Schrödinger?'

Eve and Phil shrugged their shoulders.

'A German physicist and Nobel laureate, Schrödinger advanced the mathematics needed to predict subatomic situations. In 1943, sponsored by the Dublin Institute for Advanced Studies, Schrödinger wrote a speculative book, in which he describes a flame as a "fleeting stream of order" or, in other words, as a form of organization. [3]

'I asked myself what the reality of a flame, as organization, involves. Is it in its shape, in its color, in the light and heat that it emits or in the fumes that it produces? It dawned on me that it is not in the features that we observe but in gas molecules oxidizing or burning simultaneously.'

'Why?' Eve asked.

'Well, when gas molecules no longer oxidize or burn simultaneously, the flame's observable features will simply disappear.

'Incidentally, Schrödinger added that the human body is also made up of molecules that oxidize simultaneously.'

'Flames and human bodies have more in common. They both keep the oxidation process going by themselves,' Umberto noted.

'That's right! Hang on to Umberto's observation!'

'What does oxidation mean and how exactly does it turn a flame into organization?' Eve asked.

'Well, suppose you have a cloud of methane molecules, a gas which is abundantly available on Earth. When methane molecules oxidize, they bind with oxygen molecules that float freely in the air. The binding process will take place at a certain temperature only. When the binding process occurs, heat among other things is produced which is why this type of oxidation is called burning.

'To start the oxidation process, you'll need to raise the temperature somewhere in the cloud to a level that makes a methane molecule bind with two oxygen molecules. The binding process produces, alongside heat, a carbon-dioxide molecule and two water molecules. Agitated by the heat that is released during the binding process, these molecules move away on haphazard paths of collision. These collisions increase the

---

[3] *What is Life?*, The Macmillan Company, 1945

chance of methane molecules bumping into oxygen molecules because they add to the chaos in the cloud, as it were. Of course, some energy is lost through these collisions, energy that can no longer be used.'

'Aha, you mean "entropy!"' noted Umberto.

'You are losing me! Did you say, *entropy*?' Phil interjected.

'Yes, entropy! It is the energy lost in a process, energy that cannot be recovered. It's not relevant now, Phil! We'll discuss it later on!'

Phil gracefully accepted M's suggestion.

'When the heat that is generated spreads to neighboring areas, some of the methane molecules in these areas start oxidizing too. The heat that is produced spreads further inside the cloud until entire colonies of methane molecules all oxidize simultaneously.

'You might say that oxidizing gas molecules create the behavioral space needed by other gas molecules to oxidize.'

'That is how a flame keeps the oxidation process going!' Umberto reminded the others.

'Behavioral space?' Eve asked.

'Well, in a cloud of oxidizing methane molecules, behavioral space is the environment where the conditions foster spontaneous oxidation, such as the right amount of heat and the presence of both methane and oxygen molecules on collision paths.'

'I don't get it! Can you explain that again, please?' Phil asked.

'Take a company, for example. At every level of a company, leaders try to create the behavioral space or conditions needed by employees to do the right thing and work. Similarly, oxidizing gas molecules create the conditions needed by neighboring gas molecules to oxidize.'

'Aha, I see what you mean!'

'No doubt, the flame is a spontaneously emerging form of organization as well as an example of simultaneity development, but we haven't fully exhausted this example yet. The question is what the different stages of simultaneity development are.'

'These stages may help us identify other examples, I figure!' Eve said.

'That's right! In a flame, some form of organization and simultaneity spontaneously emerge in four broad stages.

'The first stage involves an environment of relatively chaotic or haphazard behavior—in this case, the cloud of methane and oxygen molecules. Such an environment is ripe for the emergence of a form of organization through oxidation.

'The second stage involves the introduction of a triggering event. In a cloud of methane and oxygen molecules, the triggering event might be the introduction of a heat source, such as a red-hot iron rod.

'The heat source must be adequate, that is to say, a *certain inequality* between the temperature of the heat source and the temperature of the cloud is needed to trigger the oxidation process.

'The oxidation of the first gas molecule will only take place when a gas molecule and two oxygen molecules come together exactly where the heat source is located. The chance that this will take place is greater if these molecules behave more chaotically. This can be achieved simply by increasing the temperature of the cloud.

'Initially, a few methane molecules will oxidize in this stage. Then, the chaotic behavior of molecules in the cloud will push the oxidation activity over a threshold, as it were, and make it spread to neighboring regions in the cloud, albeit hesitantly.

'In the third stage, you'll see a consistent rise in the number of oxidizing methane molecules, each oxidizing molecule eagerly triggering the oxidation activity in neighboring regions through the heat produced.

'Finally, in the fourth stage, you'll see the simultaneous oxidation of entire colonies of methane molecules. The oxidation activity literally rips through the cloud as a wave or stream until it stagnates when less and less methane molecules remain.'

'I have never looked at a flame like that. I have never even observed these stages!' Eve said.

'We become aware of a flame only after it arrives in the fourth stage of simultaneity development, a stage that unfolds literally in a fraction of a second,' Umberto offered.

'Typically, we tend to view the residues of repeated stage-four-type simultaneous behavior as the reality of a flame; I mean, residues or features, such as shape, light, heat, and fume.

'However, these features are but the shimmering light on the walls in the back of the cave. The simultaneous oxidation behavior that produces these features takes place outside the cave, outside our view!'

'Would it be possible to sum this up in one sentence or am I asking too much?' Eve said.

'No, that's fine! The reality of a flame can indeed be summarized in one universal sentence.'

'What makes it universal?' Umberto asked.

'It explains all appearances of reality, as I will show later on!

'Here is the sentence. I have adjusted it for the example of the flame.'

'At a certain temperature inequality, simultaneous and congruent oxidation behavior of methane molecules emerges spontaneously inside the behavioral space created by others that are moving in sync. Such behavior leaves a visible residue in the shape of a flame.'

'That's two sentences, not one,' Umberto said.

They all laughed.

'Indeed! I broke it into two to make it more comprehensible. The first sentence describes what happens outside the cave. The second sentence explains what we see on the walls in the back of the cave.'

'Interesting!' Umberto said.

'In the first sentence, four words are specific to the example of the flame: "temperature," "oxidation" and "methane molecules." "Temperature" identifies the *type of inequality*, "oxidation" the *type of behavior* and "methane molecules" the *actors*.

'In the second sentence, only the word "flame" is specific to the example. It is the term that we use to explain to others what we observe.

'Apart from these words, the remainder of these sentences applies to all phenomena of reality.'

'Why did you include the difficult term *congruent*?' Eve asked.

'Irritating, I admit but I used the term "congruent behavior" because it means *fitting behavior*, I mean, fitting in a spatial sense.

'To fully understand what you mean by this, you'll need to give more detail,' Eve said.

'Makes sense! I will!'

Eve and Phil smiled.

'Originally trained as a solar astronomer, the American physicist, Ken Libbrecht, developed an intriguing hobby: snowflakes!'

Eve chuckled, wondering where this would bring them.

'In Nature, snowflakes grow on dust particles that float in the air. No snowflake that falls from the sky in winter is the same. First, dust particles might differ in shape, size and substance. Second, in certain regions, the vaporized water in the air and, thus, the water molecules that settle on a dust particle, may contain foreign substances as a result of pollution, for example. Third, when a snowflake grows and eventually falls, it is likely to pass through atmospheric layers with different temperatures and different electric fields.'

'What has an electric field to do with this?' Phil asked.

'A water molecule has two electric poles which will make it change its spatial orientation and, thus, the way it settles on a growing snowflake when the surrounding electric field varies. This is not unlike the way a compass needle changes its direction when you hold it close to a magnet.'

'I see. But what explains these poles?'

'A water molecule consists of two hydrogen atoms that sit on top of a much bigger oxygen atom after they have coalesced with it. The region where the hydrogen atoms are has a net positive charge and the region of the oxygen atom has a net negative charge. Because of these opposite polarities, individual water molecules attract one another not unlike magnets. Due to the two smaller hydrogen atoms, the shape of a water molecule is not round but, for lack of a better word, wobbly.'

'I understand!'

'Several scientists studied the stunning structures of snowflakes hoping to explain how these structures would come about. That's where the research of Ken Libbrecht stands out.'

'In what way?' Eve asked.

'Libbrecht managed to reproduce particular snowflake structures through a process chamber or process environment in which he could maintain the conditions at predefined levels, conditions, such as temperature, humidity, the electric field, and the purity of water.

'What did he discover?' Umberto asked.

'When growing snowflakes at various temperatures, while keeping other conditions stable, Libbrecht noticed that predictable snowflake shapes would emerge at various temperature levels. For example, at minus seven degrees Celsius, a snowflake would grow into a column-like shape. At minus twelve degrees, a delicately branched dendrite-shaped snowflake would develop and, at minus fifteen, a hexagonal or six-sided plate-like snowflake structure would emerge.

'This most interesting finding puzzled Libbrecht. What produces these consistent snowflake structures and what makes temperature the determining factor?'

'He probably studied the shape of the tiny ice crystals that make up the flake's structure,' Umberto contributed.

'Confined by established theories of crystal growth, that is probably what Libbrecht did but, as it appears, without conclusive success. The problem of this approach is that it fails to explain how ice crystals assemble. To me, it raises another question. Who or what takes on the assembly task?'

'Hmm, interesting,' Umberto mumbled.

'I believe that Libbrecht may have been conditioned by his own observations.'

'What do you mean by that?' Eve asked.

'The many videos of growing snowflakes that Libbrecht shot seem to indicate that he kept his gaze on the walls in the back of the cave.'

'Do you mean to say that snowflakes are reflections of something that we can't see, something that takes place outside the cave?'

'That's what I am suggesting!

'The observable shape or reality of a snowflake is a reflection of a spontaneously emerging, hidden form of organization that involves the simultaneous conduct of actors. In other words, a snowflake structure is but an organization chart.'

'Which actors do you have in mind?' Phil asked.

'Frozen water molecules!'

'What makes you say that?' Eve asked.

'The relation between temperature and snowflake shape!'

'I don't see how that turns water molecules into actors,' Eve said.

'The clue is in the motion-related energy of water molecules which depends on the temperature of the environment. Part of the motion-related energy of a water molecule in a liquid state is in its speed, part in its rotation and part in its vibration, the latter being a result of the movement of the subatomic parts that make up a water molecule.

'Mind you, when a water molecule settles and, thus, freezes, it moves no longer. It doesn't rotate either. It just vibrates. So, when you change the temperature at which the settling process takes place, you change the vibration behavior of water molecules only.'

Eve, Phil and Umberto looked enlightened.

'When a frozen water molecule vibrates, it wobbles as a result of its irregular shape. So, whereas the opposite electric poles of frozen water molecules ensure that they attract one another, their wobbling behavior determines how they spatially fit.'

'Do you mean like people that dance together?' Phil asked.

'That's a useful way of seeing it. The vibration behavior of a frozen water molecule indeed resembles a spatial dance pattern. Thus, when frozen water molecules have the same energy, they follow the same dance pattern. Consequently, they move into the space vacated by others that dance in step, without stepping on each others toes, so to speak.'

'So, am I right to assume that snowflake structures arise from the collective dance patterns of frozen water molecules?' Eve asked.

'That's right! The snowflake shape is a residue of a wholly dynamic phenomenon that involves the spatially opportune dance patterns of millions and millions of frozen water molecules.'

'Is this what you mean by congruent behavior?' Eve asked.

'Yes! Congruent behavior means spatially fitting behavior not unlike the behavior of people or molecules that dance together harmoniously.'

'Your mention of *congruent behavior* reminds me of the universal sentences that you used to describe the flame. Do these sentences apply to snowflakes too?' Umberto asked.

'Indeed! Here they are for snowflakes.'

'At a certain temperature inequality, simultaneous and congruent vibration behavior of frozen water molecules emerges spontaneously inside the behavioral space created by others that are moving in sync. Such behavior leaves a visible residue in the shape of a snowflake.'

'Again, the first sentence describes what happens outside the cave and the second, shorter sentence explains what we observe on the walls in the back of the cave.

'This time, five words in the first sentence are specific: "temperature," "vibration" and "frozen water molecules." "Temperature" identifies the *type of inequality,* "vibration" the *type of behavior* and "frozen water molecules" the *actors.*

'In the second sentence, the word "snowflake" is specific. Again, it's the term that we use to explain others what we observe.'

'What about behavioral space?' Eve asked.

'What about it?'

'I mean, what is it in this case?'

'When it comes to snowflake growth, behavioral space is the dance space that vibrating frozen water molecules vacate for neighboring partners that dance in step.'

'I gather that, when frozen water molecules settle and snowflakes grow, the development of simultaneous molecule vibration behavior follows the same four stages as those for flames,' Umberto noted.

'That's correct. I will come back to this later on when we wrap up our search for spontaneously emerging forms of organization.'

'You talked about the way frozen water molecules self-assemble. I now learned that congruent behavior lies at the heart of it. However, I don't yet understand the force or principle behind the self-assembly process. Will you, please, elaborate on this?' Eve asked.

'Aha, you mean *The Force*! Are you familiar with the European scientists, Henri Bénard and Ilya Prigogine?'

'Here we go again! When will it end?' Eve asked herself.

'Well, Eve, *you* asked!' Umberto thought while smiling.

'In 1900, the French scientist, Henri Bénard made a remarkable discovery when he heated a circular shallow glass dish with a thin layer of liquid uniformly from below.'

'You mean a "Petri dish," named after the German bacteriologist, Julius Petri, who first used it?' Umberto said.

'That's right!

'Bénard noticed that, after a while, the surface started to show instabilities that gradually grew into small hexagonal or six-sided shapes that filled the entire surface almost like cells in a honeycomb.

'Bénard observed that molecules in the liquid would rise to the surface in the center of each cell to shed the heat brought from the bottom when spreading across the surface to the edge of a cell. There these molecules, having wasted their heat, would be ejected to the bottom. The process would repeat itself once these molecules reached the bottom. Molecules would take up heat at the bottom when traveling to the center of the cell and then rise to the surface again.

'Whereas molecules in the liquid were moving chaotically at first, they started following orderly paths when the inequality between the temperature at the bottom and at the surface reached a certain level.'

'This must be another example of a spontaneously emerging form of organization with molecules in the liquid functioning as actors and the hexagonal, Bénard-cell structure as an organization chart,' Eve said.

'The Russian-born Belgian chemist and Nobel Prize winner, Ilya Prigogine, studied the heat transport behavior of these molecules when they followed orderly paths and when they were in a state of chaos. He discovered that the capacity to transport heat was so much better when the molecules followed orderly paths than when they moved chaotically. In other words, when the molecules organized themselves, the overall heat-transport efficiency improved.'

'Where does this efficiency gain come from?' Eve asked.

'That is the question, indeed! When chaotically moving, the molecules wildly bump into each other on their way to the surface. As a result, the way up comes at the cost of energy lost through multiple collisions. Yet, after the molecules start following orderly paths, they smoothly flow through the environment and no longer bump into each other as much. In other words, then they flow both *simultaneously* and *congruently.*'

'So?' Eve asked.

'Well, not unlike rivers that find paths of least resistance to the sea, molecules in a liquid seek the *least-energy fitting* paths in the environment that they traverse. Hence, the principle or force behind self-assembly is in the continual and unavoidable search for the least-energy fitting behavior in an environment—in this case, the thin layer of liquid in a petri dish.'

'In other words, the least-energy fitting behavior of molecules in the liquid demands that they constantly take advantage of the possibilities in their surroundings,' Eve said,

'That's right. But the way you say it sounds a bit negative while it really isn't. A more accurate and fair explanation of least-energy fitting behavior is *most energy-responsible behavior.* In other words, molecules in the liquid follow paths that drain the least energy from the collective of molecules. The choice for most energy responsible behavior by each individual molecule improves the efficiency of the collective of molecules when transporting heat!'

'Why don't you simply refer to *most energy-responsible behavior* instead of *least-energy fitting behavior?*' Phil asked.

'Because least-energy fitting behavior tells you exactly what this behavior physically involves. You should not underestimate what this means in practice. Least-energy fitting behavior is exceptionally dynamic. It requires that actors constantly adjust to an environment that they help change themselves.'

Umberto shifted in his chair.

'All things considered, it is really amazing that forms of organization emerge by themselves simply by the least-energy fitting behavior of independent actors. This certainly differs from how I would have defined "organization" in the past. If you'd consult any unabridged dictionary, you would see that the verb "to organize" means "to form into a whole especially for harmonious action."

'Considering what we have discussed so far, it is quite pretentious to assume that we or, for that matter, leaders "design" organizations to achieve harmonious action. Our examination of flames, snowflakes and Bénard's cells shows just the opposite. Organization does not determine harmonious action but *harmonious action determines organization!*'

'You make a valid point, Umberto! We'll explore what this all means for leaders and leadership later on.

'There's something that I forgot to mention. Both in the example of the snowflake and in the example involving Bénard cells, the six-sided or hexagonal shape is an essential part of the resulting organizational structure. What I'd like to emphasize is that six-sided shapes are the fruits of least-energy fitting behavior rather than the seeds of some underlying principle. In other words, six-sided shapes are reflections of *least-energy fitting* behavior patterns unfolding outside the cave.'

'I have the feeling that, as we learn progressively about what happens outside the cave, we are heading for a sea change in the way we explain and deal with our world,' Eve said.

'I am curious to know whether the universal sentences, that you used to describe how forms of organization appear inside and outside the cave, also apply to the example of Bénard's cells,' Umberto said.

'They do! Here they are.'

'At a certain temperature inequality, simultaneous and congruent heat-transport behavior of molecules in a liquid emerges spontaneously inside the behavioral space created by others that are moving in sync. Such behavior leaves a visible residue in the shape of Bénard cells.'

'Not wanting to repeat myself but the first sentence describes what happens outside the cave and the second explains what we observe on the walls in the back of the cave.

'In the first sentence, seven words are specific to the situation: "temperature," "heat-transport" and "molecules in a liquid." "Temperature" identifies the *type of inequality,* "heat-transport" the *type of behavior* and "molecules in a liquid" the *actors.*

'In the second sentence, the term "Bénard cells" is specific. It is the term that we use to tell others what we observe.'

'I guess that the notion of *behavioral space* is somewhat less obvious in this case,' Eve said.

'That's true. Nonetheless, it is not too difficult to explain. The role of each molecule in the liquid changes constantly. One role is to bring the heat from the bottom to the surface. Another is to shed the heat at the surface. Yet, another is to collect the heat at the bottom and so on. All molecules in the liquid take on these roles at some point while advancing on a path inside the Bénard cell. As they advance, they create behavioral space for the molecules that follow.'

'So far, we discussed examples that involve physical things, such as molecules, but what happens when it concerns living beings? Will they follow suit as obediently as molecules do? Eve asked.

'Your question brings me to my next example.'

The discussion partners seemed to have come out of their trance somewhat. Phil realized how much Eve's questions kept the dialogue going. The dialogue had evolved into a trialogue. Some of the people sitting nearby had shifted their chairs to listen in. Also, the waitress was still watching from a distance. She was secretively talking to a young man, probably another student. When she spoke to him, her hand would cover her mouth not to show what she said.

'It seems we might have attracted the attention of more candidate escapees,' Phil said.

'We might have. On the other hand, we might have attracted the attention of people that are seeking to tie us to the walls in the back of the cave again, hoping to restore our moral anchors,' Umberto responded.

'I hadn't thought of it that way. What you just said reminds me of the meaning of the word, *religion*. It is derived from the Latin word, *religare*, which means *to bind*,' Eve said.

'Ready for the next example?

'As the four seasons unfold on Earth, we see certain bird species migrate from one region to another. Birds migrate for energy-related reasons. In Northern regions, where the days are longer, birds have more time to feed, breed and raise their offspring. In autumn, when the daytime shortens, these bird species migrate to warmer Southern regions to sustain their chance of survival. In these regions, less energy is needed to sustain a bird's body temperature.'

'Why not just stay in the warmer regions?' Eve interjected.

'In warmer regions, the temperature in summer rises to levels where energy and time is wasted to keep the bird's body temperature stable, for example, by inactivity. At that point, the chances of finding energy-rich food and raising offspring are better in regions nearer to the North Pole where the days are cooler and longer.'

'I see!'

'Initially, a few birds may start the journey in V-formation. On their way, they are likely to attract the attention of other members of their species. Hesitantly at first, more and more birds join the group until eventually droves of birds are flocking, seemingly all at once.

'This flocking behavior not only brings birds to a region where the conditions satisfy the needs of their species but it also helps birds reduce the flapping energy required to get there. Energy savings of up to 20% are possible when birds fly in V-formation. Birds have also been shown to increase their speed by as much as 3 miles per hour.'

'Where exactly do these energy savings come from?' Phil asked.

'A bird needs to work less hard when it flies inside the pocket of turbulent air behind the wing of a bird in front. Such pockets have a slightly lower pressure than the surroundings. So a bird saves flapping energy by flying behind one of the wings of the bird ahead.'

'This phenomenon is called *slipstreaming*,' Umberto added.

'Of course, by flying in these low-pressure pockets of air, birds show least-energy fitting behavior, the pockets of turbulent air behind each wing representing the behavioral space that birds create.'

'Obviously, the leader of a flock doesn't benefit from all this. How does he or she manage to keep up with the flock?' Eve asked.

'The leaders of a flock—that is, those at the front and at the tips of a V-formation—regularly yield to successors so they are not in the way of the flock's progress.'

'Human leaders often show less responsible leadership. They have a tendency to hang on to their positions,' Umberto added.

'All things considered, there are good reasons to assume that living beings can follow suit as obediently as molecules do. Living beings too are inclined to seek a path of least resistance.

'As this example also illustrates, behavioral space is not necessarily created intentionally. It may simply be a byproduct of the interaction between actor and environment.'

'So, the crux of the matter is not necessarily in creating behavioral space but in identifying it,' Umberto observed.

'That's what the search for a path of least resistance is all about. It's to be open to what the immediate environment and the natural flow of things are ready to offer.'

'Why aren't different bird species flocking together?' Phil asked.

'Apart from bodily differences that lead to either over- or undersized behavioral space, species might well be triggered by different levels of daytime and temperature inequality.'

'I see!'

'Before you ask me again, Umberto, here are the two universal sentences but now describing a flock of birds.'

'At a certain daytime and temperature inequality, simultaneous and congruent flapping behavior of birds emerges spontaneously inside the behavioral space created by others that are moving in sync. Such behavior leaves a visible residue in the shape of a flock of birds.'

'In the first sentence, four words are specific to bird migration: "daytime," "temperature," "flapping" and "birds." "Daytime" and "temperature" identify the *type of inequality*, "flapping" the *type of behavior* and "birds" the *actors*.

'In the second sentence, the term "flock of birds" is specific. This term tells others what we observe on the walls in the back of the cave.'

'I must admit, I find it truly intriguing that a form of organization emerges by itself even when it involves living beings. Does this also apply when it concerns human beings?' Eve asked.

'Well, that brings me to my final example.'

'Then what?' Eve asked.

'Then, we'll summarize our findings and call it a day.'

They all laughed.

'Not unlike all other forms of organization, human organizations emerge spontaneously when a certain inequality emerges.'

'What do you mean by inequality in this case?' Eve asked.

'An inequality might involve a new niche in the market or a certain human inequality. When it comes to human forms of organization, I generally refer to *supply* or *demand inequalities*.'

'What do these stand for?' Eve asked.

'A supply inequality concerns a shortage of supply, for example, a shortage of a commodity or justice. On the other hand, a demand inequality refers to a certain level of unfulfilled demand, such as the demand for a commodity or justice.'

'What is the difference?' Phil asked.

'The difference is in when they occur and in the path you'd follow to minimize them. As I'll explain later on, this path is not necessarily determined by economics or, for that matter, economists.

'When a societal or market inequality develops, an entrepreneur is likely to spot it at some point. Having mustered people and funds, he or she will try to deal with this inequality.

'I am glad to hear you counted us in,' Eve said.

'Because I identified female entrepreneurs?'

Eve nodded.

'Ideally, people join an entrepreneur when they share his or her urge to deal with a certain societal or market inequality. An urge that is incompatible is in the way of spontaneous self-assembly and may produce collisions.'

'Do you mean by self-assembly: when people join?' Eve asked.

'Not really! You don't create an organization just by attracting people or by giving them a role. The marvel of organization emerges only when, after repeated attempts, people start reproducing role-inspired behavior patterns that have been shown to produce growth consistently. So self-assembly involves behavior patterns. As usual, these patterns emerge hesitantly at first. Those that yield benefits are upheld. Others fade.

Surviving patterns are improved upon and, then, reproduced to generate growth.'

'Do you mean to say that the emergence of behavior patterns is really at the heart of organization?' Umberto asked.

'Indeed!'

'What about behavioral space in human organization?' Eve asked.

'Remember Umberto mentioning that the clue of behavioral space is not necessarily in its creation but in its identification? Well, in the search for paths of least resistance, people eventually start using the favorable conditions created by leaders and peers, like birds do when they flock. So the behavioral space is in these favorable conditions. It's the space where least-energy fitting behavior is made possible.'

'So, what is the crux of human organization? Eve asked.

'The reality of human organization is in the repeated role-inspired behavior of people that work together to minimize a societal or market inequality as fast as the local conditions allow.

'Just as the reality of a flame is not only in its features, the reality of human organization is not in the chart that pictures it, nor in the building that houses it, nor in the logo that represents it. These are essentially residues of human organization.'

'What do you mean by residue?' Eve asked.

'Residue involves everything that we observe on the walls in the back of the cave—in this case, features or reflections of human forms of organization, including revenues and products.'

'Allow me to broaden the discussion of the meaning of residue. Take a fossil; is that a residue as well?' Umberto asked.

'It is in two ways! A fossil is a reflection of the behavioral marvel that created it originally. A fossil continues as a complex organization of molecules that keeps its shape within a certain range of environmental conditions. As long as this "environmental inequality" continues, a fossil remains visible on the walls in the back of the cave, so to speak.'

'I see!

'I gather, the universal sentences for forms of organizations also apply to human organization.'

'Yes, they do, Umberto. Here they are.'

> *'At a certain supply or demand inequality, simultaneous and congruent role-inspired behavior of people emerges spontaneously inside the behavioral space created by others that are moving in sync. Such behavior leaves a visible residue in the shape of a human organization.'*

'Again, the first sentence describes what happens outside the cave and the second explains what we observe on the walls in the back of the cave.

'In the first sentence, five words are specific to human organization: "supply," "demand," "role-inspired" and "people." "Supply" or "demand" identifies the *type of inequality*, "role-inspired" the *type of behavior* and "people" the *actors*.

'In the second sentence, the term "human organization" is specific. It's the term that we use to explain what we observe on the walls in the back of the cave.'

'So, you are telling us that human organizations are fundamentally the same as snowflakes?' Eve said, with a puzzled look on her face.

'That's what I am trying to convey. Like a snowflake or Bénard cell, human organizations are spontaneous behavioral marvels that exist as long as the inequality that triggers them remains. They are different in only one respect.'

'I knew it!' Eve said softly.

'Compared with snowflakes and Bénard cells, human organizations are distinct in that they develop an awareness of their own emergence.'

'Does this help?'

'If an organization is aware of its own emergence, it may develop strategies to speed up its emergence.'

'That is positive, isn't it?' Phil said.

'Sure! However, it comes at a price.'

'At what price?'

'Rather than speeding up their emergence, human organizations may also slow down and even spoil their emergence.'

'As a result of what, for example?'

'Complacency inside an organization or ego—particularly, the ego of leaders! As Umberto reminded us, leaders have a tendency to hang on to their position. Their ego often prevents them from moving on.'

'So, leaders may be in the way of the development of their organizations!'

'That's right, unfortunately!'

'Something else puzzles me,' Eve said after a while.

'Go ahead!'

'What is the role of a leader when forms of organization emerge by themselves? I thought leaders were in the driver's seat.'

'Leaders still are in the driver's seat. However, they are simply not the invincible designers of human organizations. Their role is different from what they sometimes believe it is.'

'I'd love to debate this in much more detail. I have got so many questions when it comes to organizations and leadership.'

'We will, but later on. There's so much else to discuss first.'

'I guess, it's time to wrap up our discussion. I realize that it took a while to get where we are now. Yet, now that we have completed our appraisal of forms of organization, we can fall back on a solid and, at the same time, practical framework of reference that will no doubt serve us when we continue our discussion.'

Although Eve, Phil and Umberto could only guess why this might be so, they trusted M's analysis.

'As you'll recall, we started our analysis of forms of organization in search of simultaneity. Simultaneity or rather *congruent simultaneity* governs outside the cave, where the realities, that we observe on the walls in the back of the cave, emerge. Of all the things that we discussed today, what struck you most?'

Eve was the first to offer her views.

'I never would have expected to be able to compare what happens in Nature with what happens in society. The parallels are stunning and appear to be crossing the borders of both environments and disciplines. If all that we observe as reality can be translated into a common phenomenon then there must be something in the idea. Gradually, I am beginning to feel what it might be to become an escapee.'

After a moment of thought and apparently speaking on behalf of Phil, Umberto offered his views.

'There are two things that firmly reached my consciousness. First, the realities that we observe are all outcomes of behavior patterns no matter what the actors. Therefore, *the reality, that we observe, is a reflection of a parallel world*, a world of behavior patterns.

'Through your examples, you repeatedly illustrated an increasingly familiar theme of emergence, a theme that describes how behavior patterns and simultaneity develop repeatedly. That brings me to my second point. It seems to me that the parallel word of behavior patterns that you unveiled, the world outside the cave in other words, is a world of endless and relentless emergence, a world of boundless becoming.

'The principle of energy conservation says that to spend the limited energy that we have at our disposal we need to free it up first. So, in a world of relentless emergence, the opposite of emergence must be relentless too and, if the latter means decay, so be it. No doubt, this will become visible when the stages of behavior-pattern emergence end.'

M showed traces of both foresight and hindsight in his eyes, 'This is pivotal! We'll discuss this the next time around. Thank you both!'

Some of the people that had listened in applauded spontaneously. This triggered Umberto to make one more comment.

'This must be coming from outside the cave.'

They all laughed.

'When, shall we meet again?'

After agreeing a meeting place and time, the candidate escapees went their way and so did some of the other people. When Eve looked back, M shouted, 'Feel free to bring along others!'

M, on his own now, reflected on the awkward experience of seeing his audience grow spontaneously.

'Would Eve and he be the lonely birds that would start off a flock? Would this flock be flying north or south?'

'Would you like to order lunch, Sir?' the waitress asked.

55

The Emzine Phenomenon

M had an early morning meeting in Cape Town that day. Umberto had suggested continuing their dialogue in the city afterwards. They agreed to meet in the OYO restaurant at the Victoria & Alfred Waterfront, Cape Town's iconic harbor place. Away from the Waterfront's tourist area, the terrace of OYO was situated right on the water's edge and offered an unparalleled view of the city and Table Mountain.

Coming from the N2, M took the third exit of the traffic circle near the Waterfront in the direction of what was previously the prison of Cape Town. The prison buildings now hosted the Graduate School of Business of Cape Town University. A few years ago, M had presented his findings there. OYO was the place where he had eaten lunch with one of the participants following his well-received speech.

After leaving his car in a car park that was literally carved out of the colossal rock on which the prison was built, M walked in the direction of the Waterfront. He liked entering the Waterfront area this way. It would not only bring him straight to OYO. He would also pass the statues of four formidable South African leaders: Mandela, Tutu, Luthuli and DeClerk. Having met Tutu once, M knew that their example was much greater than what these statues radiated.

M arrived at the OYO restaurant well before the agreed meeting time and, also, well before lunchtime. So he was free to select a table with the best view and room for extension, should this be necessary. Having been seated by a waiter, M indulged himself with the scenery. His mind was not on anything particular. Yet, it was ready to delve into the patterns of neuron-cluster behavior that would bring to the surface the intricacies of the world outside the cave, the world where simultaneity rules, the world of boundless becoming.

Just then, a young man approached his table. Apparently, he was not certain whether to introduce himself. So, assuming that he was one of the guests of Umberto and Eve, M rose to welcome him and offered him a seat. Once they were seated, M realized where he had seen this most familiar face before. It was the chap that had been talking to the waitress at the street café, Java, in Stellenbosch.

Before M had a chance to ask him about his interests, Eve, Phil and Umberto announced themselves. They greeted M warmly. The young man rose and introduced himself to the newcomers, which indicated that he was not one of their guests. Umberto mentioned that two more people would arrive, ex-colleagues from the University of Stellenbosch. Once seated, the group chatted while waiting for the other guests to arrive.

Next to Umberto's invitees, two more people arrived. They had become part of the audience simply because they had had tea at Java and got hooked on the discussion. When everyone had ordered something to drink, they looked at M who had listened with interest but who had refrained from taking part in the discussion so far.

'Allow me to resume our dialogue with Umberto's observation. The realities that we observe are reflections of a parallel world, a world of behavior patterns and relentless emergence. Emergence refers to the congruent and simultaneous movement of actors, such as molecules, birds, and people.'

'Will you, please, explain again what you mean by congruent and simultaneous motion or movement?' Phil asked.

'Simultaneous motion refers to events that take place at the same time. The term "congruent" tells you that events unfurl harmoniously in a spatial sense and that the actors involved move in a least-energy fitting way. Considering a flock of birds, for example, *congruent simultaneity* involves the synchronized behavior of birds, all seeking the least-energy fitting conditions behind the wings of the bird in front at the same time.'

'Thank you! By the way, is it all right if I tape our discussion?'

M nodded and continued, 'When I think of the mysterious parallel world of behavior patterns, the following question comes to mind. What does *relentless emergence* entail?'

The young man shifted nervously in his chair but refrained from making a comment.

'The beginning of what might be an answer is in the four stages of congruent-simultaneity development, that is, the stages that appeared repeatedly in the various examples that we discussed.'

'As I recall, you mentioned four stages when you talked about flames. However, you didn't explore these stages in detail for snowflakes, Bénard cells, bird flocks, and human organizations,' Eve said.

'That's correct! I only hinted at them. So let me repeat these stages while also referring to the other examples.'

'The first stage of congruent-simultaneity development involves a state of chaotic or haphazard behavior. This is a crucial state because, ironically, the degree of haphazardness increases the chance that certain behavior patterns spread.'

'Can you explain this, please?' Eve asked.

'When it comes to a flame, I mentioned that, by increasing the temperature of the cloud environment, you would agitate the methane and oxygen molecules. Of course, the more chaotically these molecules are moving, the more chances will occur that two oxygen molecules meet one methane molecule in a hot zone.

'When it comes to human forms of organization, the more roles there are in an economy or society, the more are the chances of bringing together roles that resonate.

'When it comes to a thin layer of fluid that is heated uniformly from below, the more chaotic the movement of molecules, the more chances there are of finding molecules that invite flocking behavior when transporting energy to the surface.'

'Aren't you mixing up two examples here?' Eve asked.

'I did so intentionally, Eve. Flocking behavior takes place in both bird societies and molecule societies, such as the Bénard cell. It effectively occurs in all forms of organization.'

'Do you also see chaotic behavior in a flock of birds?' Phil asked.

'Yes, this is particularly visible in the flocking behavior of small bird species. When hundreds of birds start flocking, they are flying chaotically at first. A flocking pattern progressively emerges from the search for the path of least resistance by individual birds.'

'So, you are effectively saying that our world is driven by energy-efficiency matters,' Umberto interjected.

'As we shall explore later on, that is the crux of the matter!

'A second stage of congruent-simultaneity growth unfolds after an inequality introduces itself, such as a temperature inequality, a daytime inequality, or a supply-demand inequality.'

'Is the introduction of an inequality sufficient to set off the process of emergence?' Eve asked.

'Not quite!

'Some triggering event is required that kick starts the development of a form of organization—for example, a few methane molecules that oxidize, a temperature instability on the surface of a layer of fluid, a few birds that start flying in V-formation, or an entrepreneur that identifies a market niche. Once an inequality has reached a certain level, sooner rather than later, a triggering event takes place.'

'Why is this so?' Eve asked.

'Events do not take place in isolation. There are other events, even faintly related ones, that may push behavior patterns over a threshold.'

'Then, what happens?'

'As we discussed a moment ago, chaotic behavior helps by pushing rare orderly behavior over a threshold, making it spread albeit hesitantly at first. By offering a whole host of minutely different conditions, chaotic behavior offers chances for orderly forms of behavior to develop.'

'How?' Phil asked.

'Some of these minutely different conditions may resonate with a triggering event and amplify it.'

'I recognize your reference to "orderly behavior that is spreading hesitantly at first" as the phrase that you used to describe the second stage of emergence,' Eve said.

'In the third stage, orderly behavior consistently spreads. In a cloud of methane molecules, you'll see a rise in the number of oxidizing gas molecules, each oxidizing molecule eagerly triggering the oxidation of neighboring methane molecules through the heat produced in the process. When a snowflake grows in shape, an increasing number of molecules can and will settle. The other examples even better show how this stage distinguishes itself.'

'How is that?' Eve asked.

'In the third stage of the process of emergence, you'll see that least-energy fitting behavior patterns develop albeit after repeated attempts. For example, in a thin layer of liquid that is heated from below, least-energy fitting molecule paths are established gradually. In a flock of birds, the least-energy fitting bird formation develops after repeated jockeying for positions. In human organizations, least-energy fitting roles transpire at the end of a merciless path of trial and error.'

'So, what is the quintessence of this stage?' Phil asked.

'Two things, really!

'First, numerous different behavior patterns develop inspired by local conditions that, themselves, are changing as a result of similar events in the immediate surroundings.

'Second, just like a river on a path of least resistance keeps on running to the sea, behavior patterns on a path of least resistance keep on reproducing. Other behavior patterns become extinct, as it were.'

'So, this stage really is about natural selection!' Umberto observed.

'That's right but with one important footnote. Contrary to common perception, natural selection involves behavior patterns rather than physical matters or life forms!'

'Do you mean to say that one should interpret natural selection as the natural selection of *behavior-pattern species*?'

'Precisely! Natural selection essentially involves *behavior-pattern species* rather than physical species.'

'What is a *behavior-pattern species*?' Phil asked.

'A behavior-pattern species that survives in a certain environment simply involves a "class" of behavior patterns that reproduces best.'

Phil completed M's sentence, 'because it follows the least-energy fitting paths. Right?'

'That's right, indeed!'

'Nonetheless, as the examples illustrate, the natural selection of behavior-pattern species eventually produces the emergence of physical things or "life forms" such as flames, snowflakes, Bénard cells, bird flocks and human organizations,' Eve added excitedly.

'That's right!

'Anyway, now you see how the physical world that we observe in the back of the cave can be explained by the world outside the cave, the latter being a wholly behavioral world!'

Whereas the body language of Eve and Umberto showed a sense of accomplishment, the young man with the familiar face looked tense.

'I took the liberty to attend your meeting today, uninvited. I am fascinated by the topic even after hearing only fragments at Java. May I ask, where does God come into this?'

An awkward silence followed. His question came out of the blue. Some of the listeners held their breath.

'Was M prepared for this?' they thought.

M looked at the man empathically, yet with piercing eyes.

'On the whole, religion deals with matters of behavior, both good and evil. So, if you'd seek God in the pursuit of the path of least resistance, you'd affirm the kind of behavior that improves our chances. Isn't that what good behavior is about?'

'Is that it?' the young man asked, surprised by his own bluntness.

'You may also find God in the interrelatedness of behavior patterns on all timescales, from slow to fast. Behavior patterns on one time scale may well affect behavior patterns on all other timescales. Isn't that evidence of omnipotent influence?'

'I see,' the young man answered, not fully persuaded but enough to refrain from making further comments.

Remember,' Umberto noted, 'time is a human invention. Thus, the world of timescales has meaning only in the human mind.'

The young man looked puzzled and everyone sighed noiselessly.

'Where was I?

'Of course, the fourth stage! In this stage, surviving behavior-pattern species reproduce abundantly. It is then that we genuinely become aware of the shapes that these behavior patterns produce.'

'Do you mean shapes such as flames, snowflakes, Bénard cells, bird flocks and human organizations?' Phil asked.

'Yes, indeed!

'Remember, these shapes remain visible as long as the inequalities that produced them continue. However, when the temperature rises, snowflakes melt. When you stop heating a thin layer of liquid from below, Bénard cells fade. When a flock of migrating birds reaches a region with the right conditions, it breaks up. When market niches fill up, companies disappear unless they reinvent themselves'

'You forgot to mention flames,' Eve said.

'I left flames out on purpose. Like other life forms, flames themselves produce the heat needed to sustain their existence. Flames cease to exist only when they run out of methane molecules. The principle remains the same, however.'

'From what I gather, human organizations are also able to sustain their own existence,' Umberto observed.

'They are! For example, vitamin producers and insurers may sustain and even broaden their market niche by advertisements that explain how consumers may improve their chances when they buy their products.'

'These advertisements cleverly exploit the Maslovian insecurities of people,' Umberto added.

'What are Maslovian insecurities?' Phil asked.

'Maslovian insecurities involve anxieties that people experience when they fear that certain needs may not be satisfied, particularly the needs identified by the psychologist, Abraham Maslow.'

'Needs, such as?'

'Maslow identified a primary level of human needs which includes the need for water and food, in other words, physical matters that you can't do without. According to Maslow, the second level of human needs involves the need for security, health, and property.'

'I see!'

'Of course, companies cannot manipulate the market forever. Whenever societal conditions dramatically worsen, people are bound to sacrifice their secondary needs for the sake of their primary needs. So, in the end, evolving societal inequalities determine the fate of human organizations too.'

'This reminds me of my earlier observation,' Umberto observed.

'And, that is?'

'Well, relentless emergence must have an opposite side, a side of decline or decay. I imagine, decline or decay occurs when inequalities diminish or disappear.'

'That's right!'

'Behavior patterns are bound to deteriorate when the inequalities, that sustain them, disappear.

'When they do, their visible traces on the walls in the back of the cave will go down with them,' Eve contributed.

M smiled visibly appreciating Eve's persistent reference to Plato's Cave Allegory, a captivating relic from their first meeting.

'When it comes to human forms of organization, the explanation of decline is somewhat more complex. Organizations are dependent on the evolving conditions both inside and outside. I'd like to discuss this in more detail at a later stage.'

'Let's wrap up our discussion about stages of emergence.

'No matter whether we observe physical or societal realities, even the most varied examples of reality can be reduced to the rise and decline of behavior-pattern species.'

'All examples show the same four stages,' Eve affirmed.

'The first stage involves an undetermined environment or, more precisely, a stage that is characterized by a degree of undirected or haphazard behavior.

'The second stage starts when an inequality rises in the immediate surroundings. At that point, only the faint signal of a trigger event is required to start the hesitant development of behavior patterns that seek to minimize the inequality. Literally riding on the "waves" of undirected behavior, a trigger signal may grow in strength and, then, spread.'

'So, this is why a sea of undirected behavior is so important. It essentially functions as a precondition because its waves can push a faint signal over a threshold,' Eve noted.

'In the third stage, multiple behavior patterns emerge, all trying to minimize the inequality as fast as the circumstances allow. Eventually, the least-energy fitting behavior-pattern species survive simply because they are on a path of least resistance.'

'That's when the fourth stage starts, right?' Eve checked.

'In the fourth stage, least-energy fitting behavior-pattern species reproduce as long as the inequality, that triggered their emergence, exists. So what we observe is a reflection of constantly reproducing behavior patterns. *They* are behind the things or shapes that we perceive as reality.

'Later on, I hope to explore more examples that show the universality of the stages of behavior-pattern emergence.'

'Which stage follows when inequalities vanish?' Umberto asked.

'Fading inequalities will throw established behavior patterns into disarray. They create the same conditions of undirected or haphazard behavior that you'll find in the first stage.'

'So, a new cycle of emergence may start again?' Eve checked.

'That's right! Emergence is a cyclical marvel that is fired by fading and newly emerging inequalities of a different nature.'

'What about rocks? They seem pretty solid and so unlike the alleged "behavioral marvels" that you are referring to!' the young man said.

'I understand your misgivings about the idea of a behavioral world when it comes to the solid features of a rock. However, a rock is like a snowflake. The crystalline structure of a rock involves dynamically arranged lattices of vibrating atoms that fulfill the same shaping role as frozen water molecules in a snowflake. Of course, melting a rock is not as easy as melting a snowflake. Rocks sustain their structure in a much broader range of conditions owing to more tightly packed atoms.'

'What I fail to grasp then is the cyclical nature of rock emergence,' the young man said.

'The cyclical nature of rock emergence is not obvious to us because each cycle may take millions of years but recent research has shown that these cycles do exist. Apparently, no specific rock structures or minerals existed near the beginning of the universe some fourteen billion years ago. Since that time, multiple cycles of rock formation or rock emergence produced 4000 unique crystalline structures.'

The faint smile on the young man's face seemed to indicate that he did not relate well to the quoted age of the universe. Then again, the rushed nod that followed could only mean that he had accepted the behavioral origin of things that we observe as reality.

'As you suggested at some point, the four stages of behavior-pattern emergence involve "natural laws" that explain the underlying energy-related matters,' Umberto noted.

'Certainly! I'll explore these in more detail next.'

'I was wondering whether the interaction between behavior patterns is supported by other fundamental explanations, I mean, explanations that might also be used as anchors for further research.'

'Yes, it is! My exhaustive search for an explanation of what happens during the fourth stage of emergence hinged on such an explanation.'

'Where did you find what you were looking for?'

'In the end, I found enlightenment in the work of scientists, who are specialized in complex systems and chaos theory.'

'Wait! Complex systems and chaos theory?' Phil interjected.

'In view of what we discussed so far, the answer to your question is straightforward, Phil! Complex systems are emerging phenomena that involve interacting parts, such as molecules, birds and people. So flames, snowflakes, Bénard cells, bird flocks, organizations and, even, rocks are examples of complex systems.

'Then again, chaos theory does not necessarily explain "chaos" or, for that matter, "undirected" behavior. Rather, it explains how a triggering event starts the repetitive behavior of a complex system as a whole. Of course, this is exactly what we came across in the examples that we explored. Remember the first few methane molecules that oxidize or the temperature instability on the surface of a layer of fluid that triggers the motion of molecules in a liquid or the birds that start off in V-formation or the entrepreneur that identifies a market niche?'

'I see what you mean!'

'All things considered, I believe that energy-related matters are more important,' M said pensively.

'Why is that so?' Eve asked.

'Well, they are more fundamental and *more obvious*!

'Anyway, let's mull this over for a while. In the meantime, shall we have lunch?'

Everyone agreed instantly and, as it appeared, hungrily.

Umberto called a waiter who rushed to the table. The waiter suggested that the restaurant's Caesar salad with Parmesan slivers on top might be worth trying.

Once the waiter had taken the group's order, Eve turned to M.

'Since we need to wait for the food to arrive anyway, would you mind telling us a bit more about these explanations?'

M visibly gathered his energy.

'Of course, behind these explanations lurk energy-related matters, but I'll give it a try. Mind you, some of these explanations are truly leading edge and not necessarily simple.'

Eve smiled encouragingly.

'The first stage of emergence involves what mathematicians call *open chaos*, basically a broad mix of different, typically undirected behavior patterns. Such a sea of behavior patterns is likely to produce "waves" with different lengths at multiple points in time.'

'Why is that important?' Eve asked.

'Well, that is because it is a precondition for the second stage of emergence, a stage in which a triggering-event signal is pushed over a threshold, as it were, so that it can spread. Mathematicians refer to this process as "stochastic resonance."'

Phil seemed to be taken aback by this term.

'Yes, I know what you are thinking, Phil: "There we go again!"'

She laughed.

'The term "stochastic" simply refers to matters that are driven by chance or, in other words, matters that are difficult to predict. The term "resonance" involves the adding up of two or more waves with the same length that begin at the same time. Through resonance, the wave representing the triggering-event signal may ride or travel on the back of another wave. If that takes place the weak triggering-event signal will spread and repeat its triggering role elsewhere.'

'I think I now understand why open chaos is crucial. Due to its variety of waves, it offers chances for many different triggering events to ride and spread,' Eve said.

M was visible pleased.

'You mentioned that chaos theory explains how faint signals of triggering events start the shape of repetitive behavior patterns down the line but how do they do that?' Eve asked.

'Through cascading! For example, a faint trigger signal may stir up behavior patterns, which produce inequalities in the environment that trigger yet other behavior patterns, and so on. In this way, a trigger signal will influence the shape of successive environmental inequalities or environmental niches down the line of behavior-pattern emergence.'

'Hmm, I see,' Eve said.

'In the third stage, behavior patterns emerge to minimize an inequality in the environment. As we discussed, behavior patterns on a path of least resistance survive while others, that aren't, become extinct. However, to an observer, it looks as if behavior patterns develop similar characteristics. Behavior patterns appear to be attracted to a certain pattern or "attractor," as it were. This is why mathematicians, as process observers, refer to this as "attractor forming."'

'I am curious about the next stage,' Eve said, 'especially in view of the time it took you to find research that might serve as an explanation.'

'In the fourth stage, behavior patterns repeat themselves as long as an inequality subsists. Take Bénard cells, for example. They exist as long as you continue heating the thin layer of liquid in which they appear. Of course, because behavior patterns are repeated in this stage, it is much easier for us to become aware of them.'

'Certainly,' Eve said.

'Interestingly, when new signals reach organizations with many actors, you'll see a short-lived repetition of a series of old behavior patterns before a new pattern emerges. In companies and nations, this often involves behavior patterns instilled by culture. When such a series of fleeting old behavior patterns unfurls, the natural selection of successive behavior-pattern species is hastily repeated, as it were.

'The capacity to repeat patterns from the past is not at all limited to human organizations. As you may know, neurons fire short electrical pulses typically as part of a pattern of pulses or firing pattern. Now, clusters of neurons have also been shown to reproduce series of fleeting old firing patterns when stirred up by signals from inside or outside the brain. This phenomenon serves as a leading edge explanation of how our memory functions.'

'I really do not see how this explains memory,' Eve said.

'That is because I forgot to mention that each such collective firing pattern represents a fleeting recall. Apparently, our memories are stored dynamically as repeating neuron-cluster firing patterns.'

'What makes this explanation of memory stand out?

'It explains the brain's capacity to associate. For example, a signal or firing pattern produced by our eyes typically awakens a series of old neuron-cluster firing patterns before producing a new collective firing pattern that defines the observation. So, down the line, fleeting old memories in the shape of neuron-cluster firing patterns literally help shape the essence of an observation.'

'This is truly fascinating. It shows that our thinking also involves the behavioral world, that is, the world outside the cave. The realities in our mind emerge in the very same way as the realities in our world. Only the actors differ,' Umberto interjected.

Everyone in the group seemed to share this realization. A moment of meditation followed until Eve woke up the group from its trance.

'So, what do mathematicians call this stage?'

'Well, they let themselves be inspired by what effectively takes place. When behavior patterns travel from one old collective behavior pattern to the next, they essentially move from one old attractor to the next. The mathematicians who identified this phenomenon decided that the journey from attractor to attractor behaves like an attractor itself. So they coined the term "traveling or itinerant attractor."' [4]

'Why exactly do they call this journey an attractor?'

'Because the same journey is reproduced when similar signals arrive from the eyes. To observers, the resultant series of neuron-cluster firing patterns will appear to be attracted again to the same old path of fleeting firing patterns before arriving at a new firing pattern.'

'I see! Thank you!'

'I learned from this that the realities in our mind emerge in the same way as the realities in our world, which is a mesmerizing piece of knowledge, indeed! However, the intricacies behind this are simply beyond my comprehension. I would not be able to reproduce what you just explained,' Phil said.

'I fully understand. Of course, you don't need to be able to reproduce these details to understand the essence of the behavioral world outside the cave. As long as you recognize that the realities in our world and the perceptions of reality in our mind are both emerging in the behavioral world outside the cave.'

Just then, two waiters appeared to serve up lunch. An entertaining conversation followed in which listeners shared their understanding of what had been discussed so far, which produced questions, laughs, and even a sense of achievement. Interestingly, the behavioral footing of existence failed to produce trenches of disagreement. It became obvious to M that a new grasp of our world was gradually growing inside the group. M reflected on where the dialogue might take him after lunch. When a last round of coffee and sparkling water had been served, M's eyes fell on some floating ice cubes.

---

[4] *Chaos and Beyond*, K. Kaneko, I. Tsuda, Springer-Verlag, New York, 2000

'Before we explore matters of energy, as I said we should, let's first try to label the world outside the cave more accurately.'

The group was "all ears" again.

'Our perception of reality in the back of the cave, our *existential manifold*, as it were, is not more than the tip of an iceberg. After all, no matter whether it concerns flames, flocks or rocks, we effectively only observe regularly repeated behavior patterns, visible reminders of the fourth stage of behavior-pattern emergence. On the whole, the first three stages remain hidden below the surface of an ocean of behavior patterns. Now, what is this piece below the surface about?'

Not many in the group took this as an invitation for an answer. Yet, Eve seemed to have an idea worth sharing.

'This is the way I see it. The shapes that we observe as realities in the back of the cave are essentially "written" by behavior patterns outside the cave.'

This clearly illuminated the group.

'Consequently, you might define the domain outside the cave as the "magazine" where behavior patterns do their writing. This would mean that the world outside the cave might well be called the "existential manifold magazine," right?'

'You might shorten this by using the more fashionable term "zine" instead of "magazine." The term "existential manifold zine" is more distinct, in my view.'

'Well, why not make it even more distinct by marrying the initial letters of the words "existential" and "manifold" to the word "zine." This would produce the term "Emzine." So the world outside the cave might be referred to as "Emzine." What do you think?'

'I think this is a fairly accurate label for the world outside the cave. However, the way you pronounce it does not sufficiently express the full meaning of the term, in my view,' Umberto said.

'Aha, "M-zeen!" Is that what you mean?' Eve asked.

Umberto nodded enthusiastically.

'Born close to the border of Germany, I often can't help playing the German pronunciation of words in my mind. For example, Germans would pronounce "Emzine" as "M-zaine." Should Germans be asked to put on paper what they hear then they would probably spell it as "M-Sein." Interestingly, in German, "Sein" means "being." Isn't that what "Emzine" really is about?'

'This is a captivating idea. By pronouncing "Emzine" as "M-Sein," we obtain a unique label for the behavioral world outside the cave, a label that includes the *sound of being*!'

'As long as it means more than M's-Sein!' Eve said.

'Sure!'

'In view of the fundamental role of the behavioral world outside the cave, wouldn't it be more accurate to speak of *Emzine* rather than *sein* or *being*?' Phil asked out of the blue.

Surprised, M looked in Phil's direction.

'As I'll explain later on, you are *so* right!'

Umberto offered an interesting afterthought.

'An ancient thinker from the Far East once stated, "A thing in itself does not exist and can be said to be nonexistent." I now realize how accurate this statement is. One might indeed say that things are nonexistent. After all, they are but reflections of the behavioral world outside the cave, *images of Emzine*.'

'At the same time, because a thing has causes and conditions, it can be said that it is *not non*existent,' Eve said.

'They are paraphrasing Gautama Buddha, no doubt,' someone in the group mumbled.

'This brings me to an important evaluation of causes and conditions, I mean, energy-related matters that explain why the world of behavior patterns develops as it does,' M said.

Everyone in the group appeared to be ready for this.

M kicked off the discussion with a curiously broad question.

'What makes anything happen in Nature?'

The young man shifted nervously in his chair but refrained from making a suggestion.

'Inequality! Inequality rouses behavior patterns that try minimizing it. Interestingly, by returning fruit-flies to their ancestral environment of inequalities, the evolution of fruit-flies is reversed and earlier fruit-fly species spontaneously reemerge!' Eve said.

'*How* does inequality awaken behavior patterns?' M asked.

'Isn't that explained by what physicists refer to as the Zeroth Law?' Umberto noted.

'The Zeroth Law of what?' Phil asked.

'Of thermodynamics!'

'Wow, this is fast becoming too complicated for me. What on Earth is *thermodynamics*?' Phil asked.

'Please, bear with us, Phil! In minutes, the causes and conditions of *Emzine* will become much more obvious. Don't allow these terms to confuse you,' M said.

'Okay, no problem!'

'Thermo means heat and heat involves the *transfer of energy from one place to another*. Thermodynamics is the branch of science that explains the conversion of one form of energy into another.'

'First, what are energy forms?' Phil asked.

'A crucial form of energy is motion, such as the motion of atoms in a gas, the vibration of frozen molecules in a snowflake, the motion of birds in a flock. Another form is electromagnetic radiation, which comes in waves, such as light waves, radio waves and magnetic waves. In certain circumstances, these waves appear to consist of individual "wave packages" or photons. So electromagnetic radiation effectively involves motion too, the motion of photons.'

'Second, what is energy conversion?'

'Take a red-hot iron rod, for example. When we sense the heat, several energy conversions are taking place. First, the motion of the rod's molecules is converted into electromagnetic radiation, which travels in our direction. When the radiation's wave packages hit us, they energize the movement of bodily molecules. So, at that point, the waves are converted back into motion. We sense the heat when the energized movement of bodily molecules makes our sensory neurons fire patterns of electric pulses.

'I see what you mean, kind of.'

M smiled. Umberto took up the thread of his suggestion.

'The Zeroth Law claims that energy flows from places where there is a relative surplus to places where there is a relative shortage until there is an equal amount of energy in all places—an equilibrium, in other words. Of course, these places need to be connected first.'

'So, you might also reason that the pursuit of *equality* rather than the minimization of *inequality* makes things happen!' Eve said.

'Exactly!' Umberto said.

'Either case is true, of course. Yet, how does Nature know whether an inequality emerges and how does it sense equilibrium?' M asked.

'In the world of science, it is difficult to imagine an independent agent that keeps track of all of Nature's states.'

Apparently, the young man had gathered the courage needed to utter his views.

'Why do we need to explain these matters, anyway?'

'Well, if we'd know more about what exactly stirs our world, we might improve on our world by working with it in harmony,' M said.

'I see; of course!'

'Don't forget, the realities that we observe emerge by themselves outside the cave. Accordingly, when answering the kind of questions that I asked, you should build on this premise of "self-organization." So how does Nature know whether an inequality emerges and how does it sense equilibrium?'

Everyone looked at M.

'Nature doesn't have a clue! It completely ignores these matters.'

Everyone looked at M expecting him to say that he was joking.

'Humans invented these conditions to measure and explain what takes place in Nature. However, Nature doesn't work this way.'

'Then, what exactly makes things happen in Nature?' Eve asked.

'Motion only!'

Umberto and Eve looked surprised.

'Motion is at the heart of Nature.'

'Isn't that what the ancient Greek philosopher, Aristotle, said? As I recall, Aristotle stated that "to describe being as motionless is not a contribution to science. We must take for granted that the things that exist are, all or some of them, in motion,"' the young man asked.

'I do not mean the kind of motion that you'd observe in the back of the cave, that is, the *motion of things*, all or some of them.

'The motion of things led Aristotle to the idea that a *prime mover* would be needed to explain that *things may appear to come to being from not being without qualification*.'

'Then, what *do* you mean by motion?'

'I refer to motion in the behavioral world outside the cave, a world of *motion only* and *paths of least resistance*, regardless of the actors or things involved.'

'Can you give us a practical example?' Eve asked.

'Sure! Suppose you have two identical, disconnected containers, each filled with the same amount of gas molecules. First, you create an *energy inequality* by heating up the gas in one container. So the molecules in that container will move more energetically than the molecules in the other container.

'Next, you connect the containers so that gas molecules can move freely from one container to the other. Intuitively, we expect the temperature in one container to go down while the temperature in the other increases until, in the end, equilibrium is established.

'Considering what we have discussed so far, what will happen when you connect the two containers?'

'Well, the more vigorously moving molecules in the container with the heated gas will probably move to the container with the cooler gas,' Eve said after a while.

'Why?'

'The molecules in the container with the cooler gas move less energetically. Hence, they will leave open behavioral space for more energetically moving molecules to move into just a bit longer than the molecules in the container with the heated gas. So the path of least resistance will run in the direction of the container with the cooler gas.'

'Right! Then what happens?'

'When hot gas molecules bump into the molecules of the cooler gas, they transfer part of their motion energy and, thus, make these molecules move more energetically too.'

'Then what?'

'The temperature in the container with the cooler gas rises. At the same time, the cooler container becomes more crowded.'

'So?'

'Well, when the flow of molecules from the container with the heated gas runs into an increasingly dense crowd of energetically moving molecules, the path of least resistance will no doubt reverse at some point.'

'Now, fast-forward this process. What will happen?'

'The path of least resistance and the flow of molecules will reverse repeatedly until equilibrium is established.'

'100 percent! Nothing more and nothing less!'

'The push exerted by the collective of more energetically moving molecules is an *entropic force*,' Umberto noted.

'Why?' Eve said.

'Because, it produces haphazard collisions as byproduct, a useless form of motion energy that physicists refer to as "entropy."'

'I recall you mentioned the term at Java. *Entropy*, I gather, is the fee paid for the emergence of these molecule flows,' Eve said.

'The fee in non-recuperable energy! Incidentally, sudden events are likely to influence the temperature of the environment in which the two containers are located. This might sustain the reversal of the path of least resistance and keep the situation just off equilibrium,' Umberto said.

'Thank you for reminding us that the containers are part of the greater environment where similar events unfold. This is a very crude example, indeed. In Nature, you'll find numerous such containers at microscopic and macroscopic levels. You'll find very tiny ones as well enormous stellar ones that constantly change in shape in the midst of multiple other paths of least resistance,' M said.

'So, what your example shows is that Nature unfurls entirely by itself,' the young man said.

'That's what appears to be the situation. Nature doesn't need a sovereign agent that monitors inequality and equilibrium. In *Emzine*, it unfurls spontaneously by *motion only* based on the direction provided by *paths of least resistance*. The innate ability of Nature to emerge this way is at the heart of the *Emzine phenomenon*.'

'Is this supported by scientific evidence?' Umberto asked.

'Remember, Ilya Prigogine, the Russian-born Belgian chemist and Nobel laureate for chemistry? He showed that orderly paths of least resistance emerge by themselves from chaotic molecule movement in a thin layer of liquid, then discovered indeed that it takes less time to minimize the temperature inequality between the bottom and surface of the liquid when these orderly paths emerge.'

'So, you are effectively saying that Nature does not seek to create order. Rather, it pursues the most efficient conversion of energy by blindly following paths of least resistance,' Umberto noted.

'Of course, in the process, it inevitably also produces more-complex networks of paths because it is forced to find new paths of least resistance in environments crowded with previously established paths.

'This is a topic that I'd like to explore on a next occasion. Today, I have had more than my share of your attention!'

Everyone laughed nervously, which indicated to M that he may have stretched the group too much.

'Anyone interested in making a comment about our session today?'

'At the beginning of our dialogue, I asked whether you would explain the meaning of *congruent simultaneity* again. I am happy I did because it manifested as *path of least resistance* and turned out to be the very thing that makes Nature unfurl,' Phil offered.

'I am amazed that the same four stages explain the emergence of all the realities that we observe. I am also enlightened by the consistency of explanation because, when it comes to these stages, the energy-related and chaos-related perspectives go hand in hand. We truly are onto something important!' Eve added.

'From today's dialogue, I gathered that the parallel between society and the physical world can be found in the behavioral world. I learned that you should not be afraid to bump into one another but, as a group, our focus should be on finding paths of least resistance because those better our chances of survival. It may not surprise you that I am speechless to learn that Nature develops by itself. I am curious to know what set everything in motion first,' the young man said.

Everyone laughed sympathetically.

'All the above, I guess,' Umberto said.

'What struck me most today is that the realities in our mind emerge in the same way as the realities in our world. Only the actors differ!'

These comments appeared to represent the feelings inside the group.

No Beginning or End

M was on his way by taxi to the Mount Nelson hotel in Cape Town. That's where the group had decided to continue the dialogue, a dialogue that had only started about a week ago. Somehow, the regular exchanges had intruded M's dreams. 'Why?' he wondered.

Soon after the taxi had turned into Orange Street, the hotel's entrance became visible. The driver referred to the entrance arch as the Brandenburg Gate. Even accepting the unmistakable resemblance, it was curious to hear the taxi driver flawlessly refer to a landmark in Berlin.

M was glad to have come by taxi. Cars were parked on both sides of the driveway all the way up to the hotel. After M paid the taxi fee, the driver jumped out and opened the backseat door. M stepped out and walked into the entrance hall of the century-old hotel.

'Which way to the Oasis restaurant?' M asked a receptionist.

The directions soon led M to an exquisite terrace overlooking the hotel's lush garden. M instantly identified the table that had been reserved by Phil. Every one of the OYO group was already seated.

'Am I late?'

'No, we are early!'

'We brought some new participants,' Eve said, and then introduced each of them, including a student from India, called Chandra, who mentioned that she had an interest in Indian philosophy.

'The newcomers took the trouble to listen to a copy of the OYO audio tape,' Phil said. 'So, they should be up to date.'

The newcomers smiled and gestured that they were.

Once every one had ordered breakfast, the ball was in M's court again.

'During our last meeting, we arrived at *Emzine*, the behavioral world which produces the images of reality that we observe in the back of the cave. By crudely simplifying our world to collections of connected containers, we learned that Nature develops without the help of an external agent by *motion* and *paths of least resistance.*

'On the road to a new understanding of reality we have come a long way, but we have not yet escaped from a largely static world in which apparent motionlessness has meaning; I mean, a world of connected containers that reach equilibrium only after an inequality has been introduced, a world of beginning and end, throughout.

'So, before we are ready to reexamine our world and evaluate the benefits of our newfound insight, we need to make one more stride. We'll make this stride today—that is, if you allow me too.'

Everyone laughed.

'I don't see what's wrong with beginning and end,' Eve said.

'Nothing, really! However, let's go back to our exchange about "time" at Java. Not unlike the prisoners in the back of the cave, we define time or duration by relating the beginning and end of an event to recurrent events that take place at the same time, such as transitions of night and day or the regular progression of hours. So, as a matter involving beginning and end, duration or time essentially is a human invention.

'However, in the domain of emergence outside the cave, *simultaneity* governs, that is to say, *congruent* or *least-energy fitting simultaneity.* Outside the cave, duration is utterly meaningless.'

'Do you mean to say that Nature is ignorant of whether cycles of emergence are long or short and simply rests on the development of simultaneity?'

'Precisely! To Nature, *only the present matters*. Nature blindly reacts to inequalities that emerge when cycles unfurl, inequalities that lead to new cycles!'

'So, the world outside the cave must be a world of cycles within cycles,' Phil said.

'That's right! Even the ancient Pyramid texts already refer to the divine domain as the domain of "cycles, endless in the cosmic life."'

'I now remember our conversation at Hidden Valley again. To ancient Egyptians, the King's tomb was the gate to the divine domain where "Time Great" rules. I now realize that we have identified what *Time Great* really is.'

'So, what is it?' Phil asked.

'*Time Great* refers to the waxing and waning of the universal cycle of congruent-simultaneity emergence.'

'Aha! Then, the four universal stages of simultaneity emergence (the stages that we explored at OYO) must represent the four sections on the dial of an imaginary clock that shows *Time Great*.'

'What made you say that?' Umberto asked.

'Well, to preserve our sense of identity as escapees, we'd want to know what "time" it is outside the cave!'

'How true *and* useful, especially, if you'd also find the hands of this imaginary clock,' M said.

'I am sure, we—or you—will,' Eve said.

'Considering a world of "cycles within cycles," I'd like to explore the *path of Emzine*, the endless path of behavior-pattern emergence that runs on and through all time scales,' M said.

'How should I imagine this path?' Eve asked.

'The shape of the path resembles the number 8.'

'Do you mean to say that each cycle of emergence comprises this 8-shaped path?' Phil asked.

'That's right! A cycle of behavior-pattern development starts at the bottom of the number 8 going up left to return from the right at the bottom again where the cycle restarts. So the beginning of a cycle is an end as much as the end is a beginning!'

'Then, it must explain the four stages of emergence!'

'Yes, but in a more holistic way.'

'I gather that the *path of Emzine* tells us something that the four stages of emergence don't,' Eve said.

'That's right! The path of Emzine exemplifies the interdependence between the various processes that are at work during a cycle. It also shows how subsequent cycles effectively develop.'

'Do these cycles arise on multiple timescales?' Chandra interjected.

'Yes, they do! Moreover, "only together they arise."'

Chandra nodded, quite aware of the fact that Gautama Buddha might have uttered this proverb first some 2500 years ago.

'Let's explore the bottom part of the 8-shaped path where a cycle of behavior-pattern emergence starts, ends and restarts,' M said.

'That would certainly help me grasp the crux of all this,' Umberto said, smiling.

'At the bottom of the 8-shaped path, *external* inequalities stir up behavior patterns that try to minimize them. I usually picture these inequalities at the bottom of the 8-shaped path. After all, they are at the base of the reality that we observe.'

'Of course!' Phil said.

'So, triggered by external inequalities that appear at the bottom of the 8-shaped path, behavior patterns emerge on the path that goes up to the left. At the same time, behavior patterns, that emerged earlier, may return to the bottom by means of the path at the right of the bottom part of the 8. The returning behavior patterns stir up *internal* inequalities that emerge on this path, as it were.'

'I fail to see how behavior patterns stir up new inequalities. What exactly is the idea or process behind this?' Eve asked.

'Let me start with a question first. What does a company do when it wants to minimize a new niche in the market, a new supply-demand inequality, if you'd like?'

'It would identify the necessary roles and then appoint people to fill the slots,' Eve said.

'Right! Another question. What do the orderly behavior patterns of molecules in a liquid that is heated from below represent?'

'Roles, that is, roles in the transportation of energy from the bottom to the surface of the liquid!'

'So, behavior patterns simply represent *roles*. Now, when it comes to identifying roles, you have two options. You can either give the task to one "actor" or you can divide the task and give it to various "actors" that complete the task together. Of course, if you opt for the latter, you benefit from the different skills that the actors bring to the table. So what would you do?'

'I'd probably be tempted to divide the task and identify more roles, that is, depending on the talents and skills of each actor.'

'Absolutely right! So, through the "division of labor," you improve the productive powers of labor.'

'Aha!' Chandra observed. 'You are referring to the work of the Scottish economist, Adam Smith.'

'I am referring to the first three chapters of his book *An Inquiry into the Nature and Causes of the Wealth of Nations*. By the way, even Plato referred to the division of labor "as a means to increase productivity."'

'I see,' Chandra said.

'By the division of labor, Smith figured, you increase the agility of actors when they execute sub-tasks repeatedly. Second, because sub-tasks have been handed out to others, you save time, no longer needing to adjust from one sub-task to another. Third, you invite the invention of tools and methods that facilitate the process.'

'So the division of labor is essentially about the improvement of efficiency, *about finding paths of least resistance*!' Umberto noted.

'Indeed, the division of labor is the fundamental process at work on the path that goes up to the left of the 8 because it is about the creation of new *paths of least resistance*.'

'I imagine that Adam Smith only dealt with the establishment of roles, that is, with the path that goes up to the left,' Eve suggested.

'That's what you'd expect. However, he also envisaged the path that runs down the right side to the bottom of the 8. Let me explain.

'After the appearance of roles on the path that goes up to the left of 8, new inequalities emerge *in between* the roles, that is, behavior patterns that somehow manage to return to the bottom using the path down at the right side of the bottom part of the 8.'

'I have a hard time visualizing the emergence of new inequalities,' Eve said.

'Well, when you divide a manufacturing task into subtasks, you produce new inequalities *in between* these subtasks at the same time, such as product quality-related inequalities, flow-related inequalities, resource-related inequalities, and control-related inequalities. So, to sustain the subtask-enabled paths of least resistance, you'll need to identify additional roles, such as quality assurance, logistics, material planning, and management.'

'I see what you mean.'

'Roughly, the same happens in Nature. Behavior patterns come with inequalities in between them that need to be minimized by new behavior patterns. The emergence of new inequalities in this way entails that the cycle of emergence restarts where it ends.'

'How exactly do the views of Adam Smith support this?'

'Well, Smith particularly stressed that the emergence of roles "is as much a consequence of the division of labor as its cause." Thus, the division of labor minimizes inequality by creating it on the other end of the 8. As a result, the role-producing process will go on forever.'

'Minimizing inequality by creating it?' Phil asked puzzled.

'Well, by the introduction of roles you minimize an inequality but, at the same time, you create new inequalities in between these roles.'

'Okay, I see what you mean.'

'Plato already confirms this finding when he states that "the origin of nation lies in the natural inequality of humanity that is embodied in the division of labor." Interesting, right?'

A waiter arrived to serve breakfast. A natural pause followed.

'This all makes much sense, I must admit,' the young man with the familiar face said. 'However, what puzzles me is that you call in the help of economics while, so far, you have only been relying on the help of physics. At least, that is how it appears.'

'That is one way of seeing it! Alternatively, we might also have demonstrated that physics lies at the heart of economics.'

'I don't follow you.'

'Well, the Zeroth Law of thermodynamics explains what happens on the path that goes up to the left of the 8 when behavior patterns and, thus, roles emerge to minimize an inequality.'

'That's what you discussed at OYO, right? I mean your account of the two connected containers and the entropic force exerted by the more energetically moving molecules!' Chandra said.

M smiled, visibly pleased with Chandra's alertness.

'Wow, she must have picked this up from the OYO-tape,' he thought.

'On the path down at the right of the bottom part of the 8, the First Law rather than the Zeroth Law explains why inequalities emerge in between emerging roles.'

'Please, don't forget my ignorance!' Phil said.

'The First Law is clear enough. It says that the total amount of energy does not change. In other words, when energy is converted from one form to another, only the distribution of the different forms of energy are changing. Like a financial balance sheet, an energy balance shows the proportions of the various forms of energy at some point.'

'What has this do with the creation of inequalities?'

'A lot really! As you know, inequalities involve the flow of energy. According to the First Law, the inequality total will not change. Only the distribution of inequality will change.'

'Do you mean to say that the *division of labor* is mirrored by a *division of inequality*?'

'You might say so, indeed! When Nature minimizes an inequality, it generates other, smaller inequalities at the same time.

'Of course, a small part of newly emerging inequalities is lost as a result of the entropy that is created. Remember, entropy is an energy form that cannot be reused. It is the fee paid for the conversion of energy and, thus, for the reduction of inequality.'

'I see what you mean.'

'And, so do I!' the young man added.

'On the whole, what will the bottom part of the 8-shaped path of behavior-pattern emergence bring about?' Eve asked.

'In what way, do you mean this?' M asked.

'Well, when more and more roles and inequalities are produced, what would you see?'

'You would see ever-more finely grained roles that try to minimize ever smaller inequalities, in other words, streams of roles within roles and inequalities within inequalities.'

'How will this affect our world?'

'To an observer, our world will appear to become more complex.'

'What do you mean by complex?' Phil asked.

'Humans experience the interaction between a great number of distinct roles in physical, biological and social processes as complex because they have difficulty figuring out the underlying logic. Nature, on the other hand, just acts.

'Hmm, I see,' Eve said.

'Remember the development of minerals or rocks? A rock is a physical process that involves lattices of vibrating molecules. Over a period of 14 billion years, some 4000 minerals emerged. The number and complexity of these crystalline structures is likely to grow further.

'By the way, much of the energy in the universe is still in the motion or conduct of components that have emerged so far, things like fields, fundamental particles, atoms and molecules. As the universe ages, new and evermore complex phenomena are likely to emerge when motion or conduct is converted into component.'

'Aha, "conduct is converted into component." This statement is quite to the point and worth remembering!' Umberto interjected.

'Of course, the realities that we observe in the back of the cave are produced by "conduct" in the world outside the cave!' M added.

Everyone nodded.

'The human brain is probably the most complex biological process that Nature produced, so far. It involves some 100 billion neurons or actors that are connected through many trillions of paths. Through these paths, neurons are lured into joining distinct firing patterns that play a vital role in the process that produces memory and thought. No doubt, we will see the number of distinct firing patterns increase.'

'It occurred to me that you refer to the human brain as a biological process and to a rock as a process involving molecules. Aren't these "things" rather than processes?' Phil asked.

'Well, that's what you would call them in the back of the cave. Remember, the cave prisoners do not have a notion of the true dynamics outside the cave."

'Oh, I see!'

'Society is a social process that also rests on inequalities, roles and behavior pattern species. Thus far, it evolved from isolated tribes to interdependent nation states. The latter are becoming progressively co-dependent both economically and culturally. Of course, the division of societal roles will also persist.'

'Don't you think that human kind, as inventor and creator, will distinguish itself from Nature eventually?' the young man asked.

'On the contrary, human kind wholly and willingly functions as the most complex limb of Nature in the search for novel paths of least resistance! This might explain man's obsession for efficiency. No doubt, this obsession adds to the search for paths of least resistance. It produces enabling inventions, such as evermore complex electronic circuits and communication networks.'

'I never looked at it that way.'

'What's more, Nature will accelerate the growth of its capacity to identify new paths of least resistance by fusing biological, electronic and societal networks.'

'So, we are Nature!'

'As a limb thereof, we are!'

'It appears to me that the search for new paths of least resistance through ever-higher levels of complexity is like a drift or trend that itself might be part of a cycle,' Chandra said.

'You are quite right! The efficiency-inspired growth of complexity or "order" is part of a universal cycle.'

'Which universal cycle are you referring to?' Phil asked.

'Well, I mean the developmental cycle of the universe as a whole.'

'Wow!' Phil exclaimed a bit louder than she intended to.

'The emergence of the universe is not unlike the emergence of the realities that it contains. It follows the universal stages of emergence.'

'Where do you think is the universe in its development?' Chandra asked.

As M mulled over Chandra's question, he did not fail to notice the expression of restrained anxiety on the young man's face.

'All right! Let's make a brief detour to discuss the emergence of the universe.'

The group appeared to be ready for this.

'Currently, many scientists assume the Big Bang to be the ultimate beginning of the universe. However, as I'll explain later on, it is only part of the second stage of the emergence of the universe. A triggering-event is believed to have set off an unimaginably fast expansion of a primal state of energy, which produced the universe as we observe it now.

'During this expansion, the components of today's universe were formed. According to the stages of emergence, much of the energy is still in the conduct of the universe as a whole. In other words, as it continues to expand, new and more complex phenomena will emerge when motion or "conduct" is converted into component.'

'Are you familiar with the alleged existence of *dark energy* and *dark matter*?' Umberto interjected.

M nodded.

'Does your statement "conduct is converted into component" perhaps explain *dark energy* and *dark matter* as yet-to-materialize components of the universe?

'You are losing me! What is this all about?' Phil asked.

'Astronomers today have difficulty explaining certain aspects of the behavior of stellar systems. The force exerted by the energy and matter detected in the various corners of the universe is insufficient to describe the behavior of these systems. So they hypothesized that hidden quantities of energy and matter might exist which they labeled *dark energy* and *dark matter*. Of course, this issue is still much debated in the world of physics.'

'I see! So what is Umberto hinting at?' Phil asked.

'Well, Umberto reminded us that astronomers too observe but reflections of the universe on the walls in the back of the cave. Oblivious of the domain outside the cave, they are inclined to explain the behavior of the universe based on the components of energy and matter that have visibly emerged so far. As an evolving behavioral phenomenon, however, the universe has the potential to produce new components that are not visible yet. So the *remaining developmental potential of the universe* exerts a force that should be included when explaining the behavior of stellar systems.'

'So, you are effectively saying,' "what you see is *not* what you get!" Phil said.

'You might say so!'

'How would an escapee or someone outside the cave describe the force of *remaining developmental potential*?' Umberto asked.

'I believe, we touched on this at OYO where we talked about the collective push of energetically moving molecules. The force of *remaining developmental potential* is an *entropic force*, a force that is exerted by a behavioral marvel *as a whole* due to its tendency to produce *entropy*. As we discussed earlier, when energy is converted from one form into another, part of the energy is wasted as a useless form of energy called entropy. Eve succinctly referred to entropy as the fee paid to Nature for the conversion of energy.'

'So, where were we?' M asked in search of the red thread.

'You arrived at the third stage of the emergence of the universe,' Chandra said.

'That's right. In this stage, behavior-pattern species on paths of least resistance survive while others, that aren't, become extinct. Across the universe, rare spots develop where multiple levels of roles within roles rapidly reproduce, such as in biological and social forms of organization. The emergence of a multitude of recurrent behavior patterns eventually supports the spontaneous development of memory, association and consciousness. These matters foster self-assessment, self-improvement and self-organization, each of which serves Nature in its search for new paths of least resistance.'

'Please, remind me again, why are recurrent behavior patterns so important to the development of consciousness?' Eve asked.

'A sense of difference and memory emerges when inequalities trigger series of fleeting old behavior patterns first. When inequalities trigger and sustain multiple flows of old behavior patterns this way, a bare sense of surrounding and even awareness emerges eventually.'

'Your explanation does not immediately remind one of the human brain,' Eve said.

'That's quite right. Recognition, association and memory are not the prerogatives of the human brain. These phenomena have been found to arise in biological networks, such as metabolic networks, immune networks and the network of capillary blood vessels, and in socioeconomic networks, such as an economy or corporation. Of course, this is not surprising because these networks, too, are reflections of reproducing behavior patterns outside the cave.'

'You were exploring the third stage of the emergence of the universe,' Chandra reminded M.

'Indeed! So, in the first part of the third stage, isolated spots of highly complex and rapidly reproducing behavioral patterns arise across the universe. These spots stand out by the development of a capacity to identify new paths of least resistance particularly through a growing awareness of their own functioning. No doubt, the Earth is such an isolated spot. In fact, an analysis of the history of the Earth showed that its fate was determined by a rare combination of inequalities in and around the solar system of which it is part. Anyway, this is where I think the universe is in its development.'

'So, what will happen next?' Chandra asked.

'Eventually, when the capacity to identify new niches of behavior-pattern survival reaches a critical point, you'll see it spill over to neighboring regions.'

'What is the critical point about, do you think?' Eve asked.

'I cannot give you an absolute measure of it. However, I suspect, a critical point will be reached when biological, electronic and societal networks have fully merged.'

'Why?'

'Because, at that moment, they reinforce one another to the maximum.'

'What will this mean to us as individuals?'

'The integration of biological, electronic and social networks may lead to changes at a physical level. For example, communication and support technologies might eventually be located and grown inside the brain. However, the greatest change that individuals will face is in the way they interpret their world.'

'What do you mean by that?' Chandra asked.

'Well, to benefit from a world that connects at the level of behavior patterns, no matter what the actors involved, the human race as a whole will need to become an *escapee*.'

'You mean: adopting *the way* in the divine domain outside the cave , that is, *the path of Emzine*!'

'Exactly!'

'*The path of Emzine* may well compete with "the path" expounded in religious scriptures,' the young man said.

'This is how religious leaders might perceive it initially. However, the *path of Emzine* does not rest on competition,' M said.

'Why, may I ask?'

'It hinges entirely on the search for new niches of behavior-pattern species survival—that is, new paths of least resistance. It is simply not about getting there first or about pushing something out of its niche!'

'So, it might coexist with religion?'

'I don't really know. If religion would fully embrace the search for paths of least resistance as the "Good" it might.'

'If you'd embrace such a primal tendency of Nature as the "Good" then what is the value of religion?'

'Only in the back of the cave does religion bind man. Outside the cave, "actors" do not matter. Only behavior patterns do!'

'I see!' the young man said with a helpless expression on his face.

'Maybe an answer to these questions emerges from the prospects of the universe. What will happen in the fourth stage of the emergence of the universe?' Chandra asked.

'Once the capacity to identify new paths of least resistance spills over to neighboring regions, the fourth stage begins. In this stage, the remarkable complexity of roles within roles that fosters this capacity abundantly spreads across the universe, a process that may take millions of years to unfurl.'

'How, do you figure, will this take place?' Phil asked.

'The *path of Emzine* will spread through an expansion of the highly integrated biological, electronic and social networks beyond the spots where they emerged.'

'How?'

'Essentially through space travel! This doesn't mean only *human* space travel. The HIBES networks will sort out which amalgamation of its parts is needed to identify new paths of least resistance. Initially, robotic explorers, as sensory limbs of the network, will explore ever-greater regions of space.'

'You lost me, again! HIBES networks?' Phil asked smiling.

'Of course! I mean *Highly Integrated Biological, Electronic* and *Social* networks.'

'Okay, I see!'

'This is history repeating itself!' the young man said.

'Why?' Chandra asked.

'I fear that these space explorations will end up in the colonization of space.'

'I appreciate your concern. Of course, the history of colonization emerged in the back of the cave and was driven by an interest in resources. It was like grabbing food from a sleeping cave prisoner. The exploration that I refer to concerns the domain outside the cave. The *path of Emzine* is not about resources but about the identification of new niches of behavior-pattern species survival, new paths of least resistance. It's about conduct rather than competition,' M said.

'I now better understand why the adoption of the *path of Emzine* is a critical point in the emergence of the universe,' Chandra said.

'*The path of Emzine* is the gateway to the third stage.'

'That brings us to the fourth stage.'

"In the first half of the fourth stage, the orderly paths of multiple actors will become evermore visible throughout the universe. Energy forms are converted on a massive scale, each conversion being "paid" through the creation of a useless form of energy.'

You mean *entropy*, of course,' Phil added.

'Indeed!'

'Today, we can already observe the orderly paths of multiple actors. So what makes the fourth stage different?' Eve asked.

'The fourth stage distinguishes itself in at least three ways. First, a much greater complexity of roles within roles emerges. Second, this complexity is capable of minimizing ever more finely grained inequalities. Third, the complexity of roles within roles, which rests on behavior-patterns, is increasingly aware of its own emergence. It develops a novel ability to predict and affect multiple paths of emergence.'

'Do you mean something like a *celestial consciousness*?'

'I mean not just that but also a celestial ability to anticipate.'

'A celestial ability to predict, in other words?'

'Indeed! In the fourth stage, a celestial consciousness develops which includes an awareness of self, an advanced understanding of the state of the emergence of the universe, a more articulated view of the future, and a genuine capacity to identify and decide on novel paths.'

'I figure that the stages of behavior-pattern emergence are at the heart of a celestial view of the future,' Chandra noted.

'As much as they are at the heart of my view! Yet, the celestial understanding of stages of emergence will be much more profound.'

'Is our current understanding of the four stages of emergence sufficient to predict matters of emergence too?' Eve asked.

'It is! I will discuss our ability to predict in detail later on.'

'When you talk about a celestial consciousness, I can't help being reminded of the divine,' the young man said.

'The second half of the fourth stage and the stage after that will probably provide more clarity on that.'

The spirits of the young man seemed to be on the rise again.

'As the universe continues to expand in the second half of the fourth stage of its emergence, the quantity of entropy, a form of energy that can no longer be converted, will one day exceed the quantity of all other forms of energy. Then less and less energy will be converted and less heat produced.

'Then what?' Eve asked.

'The universe will simply cool. This stage is sometimes referred to as the Big Freeze. Of course, when less and less energy is converted, the behavior patterns involved in the conversion process will fade and so will the celestial consciousness that rides on these.'

'So, that's the end?' the young man asked.

'No, it is the first stage of a new cycle of emergence.'

'Of the universe?' Phil said.

'Indeed! The first stage culminates when the universe, full of non-converting energy, is short of the behavior-pattern species needed to sustain itself.'

'How will the process of emergence restart?' the young man asked.

'Well, a universe dominated by a form of energy that rests on haphazard behavior rather than on the conversion of energy is short of the behavior patterns needed to sustain its spatial magnitude. As a result, it will begin to collapse. When that takes place, the second stage of a new cycle of emergence starts.'

'Then what?' Eve asked.

'The second stage starts with a long and colossal contraction that gains in speed due to an increasing pull from a growing center. It is followed by a formidable implosion in which established behavioral features are brutally smashed. This colossal contraction is sometimes referred to as the Big Crunch. However, this is not where it ends.

'What do you mean by that?' Eve asked.

'Well, this is an exceptionally dynamic event that involves pure motion in the end. Not unlike balls that bounce back against a wall, the shock waves of contraction that collectively hit the center might eventually bounce back with nearly the same incredible speed at which they arrive. That's when another Big Bang or, rather, Big Bounce occurs.

'What happens then?'

'You'd see the emergence of behavior patterns that tread the path of behavior-pattern emergence exceptionally fast initially. So the division of labor and inequalities as well as the natural selection of behavior patterns would continue. Some of these behavior patterns would survive and sustain themselves. One of these might involve a universe like the one that we occupy.'

'Do you mean to say that we are part of a multi universe or "multi-verse" rather than a universe?'

'That might well be the case, at least, initially. Remember, on all scales, behavior patterns follow the *path of Emzine*.'

A brief silence followed when the group mulled over the prospect of a celestial consciousness that might emerge to fade.

'What is the purpose of a celestial consciousness that is destined to disappear?' the young man asked after a while.

'Its purpose is to pursue the *path of Emzine*. The reason for its emergence, its real destiny, is to sustain the completion of the fourth and probably longest stage in the emergence of the universe.'

Clearly moved by the *path of Emzine*, Chandra turned the matter around. 'So, rather than end, the universe will be contracting and expanding through cycles that will continue forever.'

'That is what it effectively boils down to!'

'The repeated expansion and contraction of the universe is Nature breathing. Celestial consciousness emerges when Nature exhales. Breath gives life! How palpable an image!'

The young man appeared to share Chandra's wonder.

'This is inspiring, to say the least. The illumination by the divine domain outside the cave where behavior-pattern species rule has made the veil of divinity less opaque to me.'

'To be frank, I do not see much room left for the divine other than symbolically perhaps,' Phil said.

The young man smiled deferentially.

'I believe this might be a good time to have tea and cake,' Umberto suggested. Everyone sighed, M included. Phil asked a waiter to take the order. After tea was served, they sipped and brooded.

'Let's now discuss the top part of the 8-shaped path of behavior-pattern emergence,' M said after tea.

Eve looked at M, admiring his stamina.

'After all this, how can the top part make a difference?'

'You'll be interested to learn more about the top part because it not only expounds the idea of Emzine but also the emergence of celestial awareness.'

'I see! So what happens in the top part?'

'After behavior patterns emerge on the path on the left side of the bottom part of the 8, they move up and cross to the right side where the top and bottom part of the 8-shaped path meet. On the top-right trajectory, least-energy fitting behavior patterns start out reproducing patterns that have less of an energy advantage.'

'Is this what "natural selection" is essentially about?'

'Indeed, behavior-pattern species that out-reproduce others due to their energy advantage are behind the process of natural selection.'

'I imagine that these least-energy fitting patterns will reach the top of the 8-shaped path of behavior-pattern emergence. So, as they keep on reproducing that is when and where we'll become aware of them as "things,"' Chandra suggested.

M nodded in agreement.

'I assume some other law is involved here,' Umberto said.

'You're right, the Second Law of thermodynamics! It predicts that a useless form of energy or entropy is produced as byproduct when behavior patterns convert energy to minimize an inequality.'

'I really don't see how this explains the natural selection of least-energy fitting behavior patterns,' Eve said.

'On first sight, it doesn't—that is, not without the findings of the Nobel laureate and chemist, Ilya Prigogine. Prigogine demonstrated that Nature tries to minimize inequalities as fast and, thus, as efficiently as local conditions allow. In other words, he proved that the Second Law is not just about entropy creation but also about the prevalence of least-energy fitting or most efficient behavior patterns.'

'Does this explain why birds seek least-energy fitting positions in a flock when they migrate as a group?' Eve asked.

'That's right! When it comes to rivers, flames, snowflakes, flocks or business organizations, actors, no matter whether they be molecules, people or birds, are inclined to make use of the behavioral space created by others when collectively trying to minimize an inequality.'

'Why is that again?' Phil asked.

'Well, behavioral space is the space where least energy is needed.'

'Is that why it pays to be lazy at times?'

M smiled.

'To conclude, due to their energy advantage, least-energy fitting behavior patterns out-reproduce and, thus, survive behavior patterns that are not on a path of least resistance. This is what natural selection is fundamentally about.'

'What happens when you follow the 8-shaped path of behavior-pattern emergence over the top down the left side?' Eve asked.

'This is perhaps the most interesting part of the *path of Emzinepath of Emzine*. Because no new inequalities are introduced on the path that has been followed so far, the least-energy fitting behavior patterns keep on reproducing or repeating themselves as they continue on their way from the top left all the way down to the bottom right of the 8-shaped path. Just about where the top and bottom parts of the 8-shaped path cross, they'll meet more recent behavior patterns that are following the path up from the bottom left of the 8-shaped path.'

'What makes this so significant?'

'It has an astonishing side-effect. Repeating or reproducing behavior patterns are recollections or reflections of past inequalities. When these reflections meet more recent behavior patterns, a sense of past and present, if not context, emerges. So this is where and when awareness begins.'

'That reminds me of how time is established in the back of the cave! Motion invited itself to be translated into repetitive behavior patterns here,' Umberto offered.

'To me, this also means that consciousness is not a prerogative of humankind. In the domain outside the cave, the seeds of awareness are literally at the heart of the idea of Emzine!' Chandra observed.

The group seemed to agree with Chandra on this.

'Of course, at the bottom right of the 8-shaped path, new behavior patterns emerge to minimize inequalities in between the constantly reproducing behavior patterns that arrive from the top left.

'Behavior patterns, that newly emerge due to internal and external inequalities, mix with the reproducing patterns. Together with the newly emerging behavior patterns, the reproducing behavior patterns reenter the process of natural selection further up the path of the 8. As a result, Nature's sense of distinction inevitably becomes increasingly faceted. Thus far, this has culminated in human awareness.'

'I now understand how and why celestial consciousness may arise at some point,' Eve noted.

'Wait a minute! I'd expect the process of natural selection to sift out behavior patterns that are not on a path of least resistance. As a result, behavior patterns are lost in the process and can no longer contribute as "recollections." Right?' Phil interjected.

'That is too narrow an interpretation of natural selection. Behavior patterns may survive in "neighboring" niches with slightly different conditions where they continue to influence the process of natural selection on the *path of Emzine.*'

'I have difficulty imagining what you just said.'

'Well, a helpful example is the growth of snowflakes in Nature. As I mentioned at Java, no snowflake that falls from the sky in winter is the same. Each flake traverses various atmospheric layers where the conditions, such as temperature and humidity, differ. Depending on the conditions, only water molecules with certain vibration patterns make it in the settling process. However, when these water molecules settle, they do not just shape the structure of a snowflake. Through their vibration behavior, they also influence the chances of future settling candidates whose vibration patterns must somehow fit too.'

'I see! So the vibration patterns of the water molecules that have settled on a snowflake are reflections of the atmospheric layers that the growing flake passed through.'

'That's right! You might say that the structure of a snowflake is a souvenir of the atmospheric layers that the flake once traversed.'

'Of course, this applies to snowflakes that maintain their shape but not to rivers.'

'On the contrary, reflections of previous behavior patterns are in the paths that rivers follow and in their current state of turbulence. When it comes to river paths, just visit the Grand Canyon!'

'I never thought about it like that!'

'An even more dynamic example of natural selection can be found in the human brain. As I mentioned earlier, neuron-cluster firing patterns tend to reemerge temporarily when a new signal from the sensory organs arrives. In this way, previous neuron-cluster firing patterns help select or shape future neuron-cluster firing patterns.'

'So, everything we do leaves behavioral traces, traces that help shape the behavior patterns of the future,' the young man said.

'This is what the *path of Emzine* is about and this is what gives meaning to our existence and life.'

'We have a come a long way this stretch. Today, we discussed, to some extent, what the world outside the cave is about.

Chandra was the first to offer her thoughts about what would later be referred to as the "Mount-Nelson Exchange."

'This is the first time that I attended and I am genuinely inspired by the world outside the cave, a world worth escaping to, in my view. Considering especially the culture in which I grew up, the idea of a world of cycles within cycles responds to my hunch about the true nature of Nature.'

'The explanation of the *path of Emzine* meets my expectations as an engineer. As an explanatory device, it depicts the basic processes of emergence and neatly brings in the laws of thermodynamics. No doubt, the magic of this concoction is in its universal application and in what it might help us accomplish,' Umberto added.

'I am moved by the natural way in which "celestial intelligence" might develop. I could not have guessed that I would be able to see the coming of a higher form of intelligence one day,' the young man said.

'Not so long ago, this was completely beyond my reach. There is so much that I now understand better,' Phil said.

'I realize that some of you may have become an escapee like me. The crucial question ahead of us is how the knowledge of the world outside the cave will affect the world in the back of the cave. That is what I'd like to explore with you from here.'

A New Experience, A New Science

It was one of those fine Sunday mornings when from all directions, narrow streams of calmly chatting students approached the little white church at the heart of Stellenbosch.

When nearly all the church pews were occupied, Abigail hurriedly arrived, her white dress crinkling each step she made. Standing in the doorway, she searched for the familiar face of Zander, the young man she had met in one of the philosophy classes this trimester. She was his senior by a year. This might explain why she felt a need to care for him, a need that, so far, had been unanswered. He was *so* independent.

Of all the young men present, he was the only one who turned around to check the church entrance. When Zander's eyes found Abigail's, she tiptoed towards him to take the seat that he had kept free for her. Her hand touched his in a way that was more than casual. Just then, the church organ started to play and the minister made his entrance. Unlike other times, the magic that Abigail experienced was not in the collective sense of devotion but in the presence of the young man standing next to her.

As the service progressed, she could not but notice his air of detachment, not towards her but towards the texts that were uttered and the hymns that were sung. She noticed it but, under the spell of his presence, she failed to pursue the matter in her mind. When the service came to an end, they merged with the crowd and left the church. After the flock dispersed, Abigail and Zander were on their own.

'I am scheduled to work at Java this afternoon. So why not have brunch together in the Botanic garden?' she said.

'Sounds like a great idea.'

'If you don't mind, I'll put on another dress first.'

'No problem! Shall I go to the Botanic garden and meet you there?'

'No, it'll only take a minute. Come!'

Abigail shared a room on the Van Riebeek Street not far from the Botanic garden. When they arrived at the dormitory, it was deserted and so was her room at the first floor.

'My room mate is visiting her parents this weekend,' Abigail said.

When Abigail went into her room, Zander politely waited outside but she gestured him to follow her.

'Come!' she said.

The moment she turned the door key, he saw her transform from a composed theology student into a fertile feminine phenomenon that put her arms around his neck. For a moment, he was taken aback.

Not long thereafter, they left the dormitory and walked hand in hand to the Botanic garden on the corner of Neethling and Van Riebeek. They went straight to the friendly garden restaurant and found a table in the shade of an age-old blue-gum tree that functioned as the restaurant's natural canopy. Once they had ordered, the talking really started. Asking question upon question, they sounded each other out on many topics, from their favorite color to the meaning of their first names.

'Zander, what does it stand for?' Abigail asked.

'Protector!'

'What I wanted to tell you,' Zander added, 'is that I attended two more meetings of the people that you pointed out to me at Java.'

'Remind me again!'

'Well, remember the lady and gentleman who debated these rather philosophical matters, an exchange that spontaneously drew people at tables nearby into the discussion?'

'Yes, I remember now. What about them?'

'Well, I am very grateful for your suggestion to make use of their open invitation to join their next gathering.'

'Why is that?'

Zander told her about the meetings that he attended at OYO and Mount Nelson, about the growing number of participants, about the "path of Emzine," about the remarkable depth of the findings and how these had touched his inner views about the nature of Nature.'

'After learning about these findings, I must admit, there is less room left in my mind for the divine. Strangely enough, the "path of Emzine" deepened my sense of spirituality and awareness.'

Abigail looked at Zander as if a falling branch had hit her.

'Is it a temporary aberration in his beliefs or is it because he majors in philosophy?' she thought.

'I now understand why you looked so distracted during the service this morning. I couldn't think of a reason why but now I see! How can you doubt a phenomenon that inspired humanity for thousands of years?' Abigail reacted angrily.

'I don't doubt God, Abigail. He is real in the mind of the beholder. He also came to the aid of his creators, scribes, such as those of the ancient Hebrew leaders and the Mesopotamian King Hammurabi, who sought to legitimize the Ruler's code of conduct by calling in the help of the divine.

'My recent learning is not based on denial but on a novel insight into the nature of the world outside the cave, a world that, not unlike the domain of the divine, is beyond our view.'

'I lost you on the very day I got you,' she nearly cried.

'Who will give direction in your life?'

'You didn't lose me, Abigail, not unless you want to. When it comes to direction, what direction do you mean?'

Abigail shrugged hopelessly.

'If you mean direction in the way of conduct then, let me assure you, the *path of Emzine* is just about that, yet more objective, open-minded and serene than the carrot and stick of religion. Why don't you join me when the group meets again?'

'Me joining pagan practices? This would go against the grain of my Christianity!'

'Don't forget you are a student! Considering your studies, it might even be useful.'

She stared sorrowfully at the crown of the blue-gum tree.

'By the way, the topic is not religion but the effect of this novel insight on civilization. The intention is not to replace someone's beliefs but to add to them,' Zander added.

'Very kind of you to offer us a lift!' Eve said from the back of the car. She was sitting next to Phil who gave her front seat to M.

'Thank you both, indeed!' M added. 'By the way, which route will you take to Noordhoek, Umberto?'

'The Chapman's Peak Drive from Hout Bay! Who can resist such a spectacular view of the Atlantic Coast?'

'The scenery is well worth the numerous curves on this route,' Phil added.

'No doubt about that,' M replied, enjoying the view as he spoke.

Everyone in the car seemed to agree that, when you finally arrive at Noordhoek this way, it feels like entering Paradise. Surrounded by the foothills of Table Mountain, the lush green Noordhoek area is enclosed by a pristine West-facing beach which offers a fabulous sunset every evening. The plan was to meet for lunch at the Foodbarn Restaurant right in the middle of the Noordhoek Farm Village and just a few minutes from the beach by car.

Rather than continuing on the road as the signposts indicated, Umberto turned right towards the beach.

'Aren't you missing that sign, Umberto?' M asked.

'No, I am not. Thanks! Phil arranged for everyone to meet at the beach first.'

'The view and ocean waves are so beautiful there that I thought it would be a good idea to start with a short stroll on the beach,' Phil said.

'What a great initiative!' M exclaimed.

Not long thereafter, they reached the parking area and got out. As they walked towards the beach, the sound of rushing waves became stronger every step. When at last the sea came into view, the placid broadness of the beach stirred a sense of freedom that would make a horse gallop beyond the horizon. The group was already waiting for them at the water's edge. Hellos were exchanged. Again, the number of people present amazed M. The young man with the familiar face was one of the first to approach him.

'Sir, I haven't had a chance to introduce myself properly. My name is Zander and this is my friend.'

'Good meeting you, Zander! "Protector," right?'

Zander couldn't believe his ears. This was the first time that someone knew what his name stood for.

'How do you know, sir?'

'I just happen to know, Zander,' M said smiling.

Abigail looked at M as he was chatting with Zander. From what she remembered after seeing him at Java and based on what Zander had told her, she'd expected him to be much taller. M seemed to compensate for this by showing a sincere interest in the people that he spoke to. Then M turned to her.

'Hi,' she said and offered to shake hands. 'I am Abigail.'

'Hi! How are your theology studies going?'

'You still remember, do you?'

'Of course I do. Are you happy with the progress you are making?'

She overcame her shyness and gave him a short update of what she'd achieved so far and what she had ahead of her. He listened as if she was talking to him in private. She soon realized that she couldn't keep him much longer as other people had gathered to speak to him.

Abigail noticed that one of them wore a kufi, a headdress for Islamic men. He introduced himself by the name of Abdul. M responded with the question whether he was named after "Abû Bakr." She smiled when she saw the surprise on the man's face. Apparently, M knew the name of Muhammad's rightful successor—that is, according to the Sunnis— whose full name is *Abdullah Ibn Abi Qahafa*. M listened to him with the same intensity. She also heard a physicist by the name of Gabi introduce himself. Judging by his accent, he was an Englishman.

Eventually, it was Phil who addressed the group to get things going. She welcomed everyone and explained that all the newcomers had taken the trouble to listen to the tapes of the sessions at OYO and Mount

Nelson. She noted that the transmission of the Emzine ideas had consumed much of her time and could grow into a cottage industry. Together with Umberto and Eve, she was working on a summary of the sessions at Hidden Valley and Java. She finished her update with a reminder about the logistics because the actual session would take place at the Foodbarn Restaurant later on.

Then, the "Noordhoek Stroll" or what would later be referred to as "the Stroll" began. The group walked quietly along the seashore. The sound of clashing waves stimulated an almost touching sense of tranquility. Not many talked and those that did talked in a subdued way. At some point someone, it was not clear who, asked M about the *path of Emzine*. Would he summarize it again?

M stopped and searched for a piece of wood to draw in the sand with. Within minutes, a twig, the size of a cane, was handed to him and M walked closer to the sea to find a clean slate of wet sand.

'The *path of Emzine* explains the primal process of emergence that sustains our world at every level and on every timescale. Perhaps the best way to explain the *path of Emzine* is to experience it by *walking it*. Imagine an 8-shaped path that you'd follow starting from the bottom of the 8 going up left. As I pointed out at Mount Nelson, the *path of Emzine* follows the outline of the number 8. The question is what would make anything in Nature follow the *path of Emzine*.'

M drew a triangle in the sand.

'This triangle is the Greek letter, Delta. It refers to "change" and represents the "inequality" that change produces. The *path of Emzine* starts at the triangle where an inequality rouses behavior patterns that try to minimize it.

'Please, follow me one by one! When you do, assume that you are a behavior pattern. As you know, the *path of Emzine* applies no matter who or what the actors involved! By the way, do not step on the triangle because it functions as our reference point!'

Starting from the triangle, M walked parallel to the sea following the left side of the bottom circle of a large imaginary 8. Halfway up the bottom circle, he stopped and so did the people that followed him. Most of the people were still waiting to join near the triangle.

'As we walk along the left side of the bottom circle of the number 8, each of you, as behavior pattern, plays a role in the minimization of inequality. This is where *the division of labor* takes place.'

M paused and made sure that everyone was on board.

'What is at the heart of this imaginary circle?' M asked rhetorically. 'Remember, *motion* is what makes things happen in Nature. So motion is at the heart of the circle.'

M wrote a capital letter, M, at the heart of the bottom circle.

No doubt, it might have occurred to some in the group that this letter directly or indirectly referred to M himself. I assure you, if someone had suggested it, he would have denied it rather bluntly.

'Let's continue our walk to the top of the bottom circle.'

As M and his followers slowly walked along the outline of the imaginary circle, they made room for others still waiting to join near the triangle. When M stopped at the top of the bottom circle, a chain of people marked the left part of the bottom circle.

'Where I stand now is where the bottom circle of the imaginary 8 touches the top circle. I'll continue up the right side of the top circle just as you would when you write an 8.'

Halfway on the right part of the top circle, M stopped again. By now, the chain of people meandered all the way back from where M stood to the triangle where people were still waiting to join.

'On the right side of the top circle, just about where I stand, least-energy fitting behavior patterns out-reproduce and, thus, survive behavior patterns that have less of an energy advantage. So this is where *natural selection* takes place.'

'Now, let's assume that each of you represents a least-energy fitting behavior pattern so everyone can follow me as I continue.'

When M and his followers arrived at the top of the imaginary 8, he stopped again and drew a square with quadrants.

'This square and its quadrants symbolize the features of the four stages of emergence that we identified in the back of the cave. This is the only part of the *path of Emzine* that we effectively observe.'

'So, at this point we see reproducing behavior patterns that maintain their basic structure or shape, right?' Phil asked.

M acknowledged Phil's observation.

'The *path of Emzine* continues down the left of the top circle until it arrives where the top and bottom circles of the imaginary 8 meet.'

When M started his way down, the remainder of the people that had been waiting near the triangle had finally joined. The chain of people, which now traced back all the way to the triangle, showed almost three quarters of the outline of the imaginary 8. When M arrived at the bottom of the top circle, he had no option but to stop because the last part of the human chain, that was on its way up on the left side of the bottom circle, blocked the way.

'Do you see what happens here? At this very point, reproducing behavior patterns meet more recent behavior patterns that are arriving from the bottom circle.'

'So, this is where the past and present meets!' Eve said.

'Indeed! Reproducing or repetitive behavior patterns are reflections or memories of inequalities that emerged in the past. So, when these meet behavior patterns produced by more recent inequalities, a sense of awareness or past and present emerges.'

'This is also where motion can be translated into repetitive behavior patterns to establish *time*!' Umberto added.

'Then, what is the top circle about?' Phil asked.

'It is fundamentally about *memory*!' M said while writing a capital letter, M, at the heart of the top circle.

'I would have guessed the top circle to be about *natural selection*,' Phil said, surprised.

'*Natural selection* and the *division of labor* are process labels that were invented in the back of the cave. Nature does not select or divide anything! It acts and, when it acts, it takes paths of least resistance.'

'Yet its actions hinge on motion and memory,' Umberto noted.

'I cannot agree more.'

'It is captivating to learn that memory is just as crucial to Nature as motion. Celestial consciousness *is* truly natural!' Zander said.

M smiled and nodded.

'Here my followers and I, as reproducing behavior patterns, cross the juncture to the bottom right of the 8-shaped path of behavior pattern emergence. On the bottom-right stretch, new behavior patterns will arise to minimize the inequalities in between us. You might refer to these inequalities as "internal" inequalities.'

'I guess, these internal inequalities are more finely grained,' Phil said.

'Indeed! This is where the *division of inequality* takes place.'

'Of course!'

'So, should my followers and I continue past the bottom of the 8 to the left of the 8 again, we would mix with behavior patterns that emerge to deal with *internal* and *external* inequalities. Further down or, rather, *up* that path, we, as reproducing patterns, would reenter the process of natural selection where we'd compete with them.'

'Of course, this competition essentially involves the survival of least-energy fitting behavior pattern species, right?' Chandra noted.

'That's correct!'

When everyone in the group had completed the *path of Emzine*, they gathered near the triangle again. The 8-shaped path of footsteps between the triangle and square with quadrants was clearly visible and so were the capital letters M.

'Does this answer your question?' M asked.

Everyone in the group nodded in agreement.

'Observed vertically, the *path of Emzine* follows an 8. For what ever it is worth, the number 8 signifies success in China. More markedly, if you'd picture an 8 horizontally, it represents the sign for infinity in mathematics. Of course, like Nature, the *path of Emzine* is infinite.'

'How appropriate!' Chandra noted.

Just then, an unexpectedly large wave clashed on the beach and ran towards the group. Warned by Eve, the group retreated just in time. However, the triangle, quadrants and the 8-shaped path were instantly washed away. Only, the 2 M's were still faintly visible.

'Apparently, Nature has been watching us. It wants to remind us that the *path of Emzine* belongs outside the cave,' M said with a smile.

'Anyway, I am surprised by the clarifying power of this symbolic experience of the *path of Emzine*. It may be well worth repeating this with others.'

The group appeared to share M's observation.

'I suggest we head for the Foodbarn and continue our discussion there,' Phil said, looking at her watch.

On the way back, the group talked about the collective experience of the *path of Emzine*, a path that is real and unreal at the same time.

'You are right, Zander! This doesn't appear to be about religion. I saw a genuine admiration for Nature instead. I am now starting to understand your deepened sense of spirituality and awareness,' Abigail said on the way back.

Zander looked at her and smiled.

'Interestingly, the *path of Emzine* explains our world as a behavioral marvel. This is why it may touch religion after all,' Abigail added.

'How's that?' Zander asked.

'Ultimately, religion is about improving, if not influencing, people's behavior and even thinking!'

'I see! Well, if the *path of Emzine* explains our world, wouldn't you expect it to explain religion too?' Zander said.

'Hmm, I didn't think about it that way.'

The creation of Franck Dangereux, a French Michelin-starred chef whose travels across the world eventually brought him to Cape Town, the Foodbarn is a shed that has been transformed into a restaurant. The combination of informality and quality has turned the Foodbarn into a place that everyone in the group seemed to appreciate.

Phil had preselected a light lunch menu. So the food was served soon after the group arrived. Eventually, when everyone had finished, M opened the discussion.

M welcomed everyone and thanked particularly Phil for taking on the organizing task. He also thanked Umberto, Eve and Phil for their efforts to facilitate the transmission of the *path of Emzine*.

'The purpose of our gathering today is to evaluate the effect of the *path of Emzine* on science. I'll start with a summary of how the *path of Emzine*, as an "outside-the-cave" worldview, distinguishes itself from the traditional "back-in-the-cave" way of explaining our world. So what, according to these two world views, is reality really about?'

M looked around the group to gauge their readiness.

'When it comes to the worldview in the back of the cave, "Reality" typically involves matter—I mean, physical things that interact at different levels, such as elementary particles, atoms and molecules as well as forms of organization that use these as components, such as organic substances and, even, human organizations. Of course, as Einstein demonstrated, matter is on a par with energy. So, in the back of the cave, "Reality" includes forms of energy, such as radio waves, magnetic fields and light. On the whole, science explores, explains and classifies the interaction between these most observable things.'

M saw Umberto and Gabi nodding.

'The reality outside the cave is an entirely different cup of tea. The idea behind Emzine is that reality is sustained by behavior patterns. In other words, reality is not a physical phenomenon but a behavioral phenomenon. The physical reality that we observe in the back of the cave is just one stage in the development of behavior patterns, a stage in which behavior patterns abundantly reproduce so that we cannot but observe them. Briefly, according to the worldview outside the cave, the texture of reality consists of behavior patterns that are on an endless path of emergence and, thus, as the *path of Emzine* also illustrates, reality is not about being but about *becoming*.'

'Then, how do you explain the stagnant solidness of this wooden table, for example?' Abigail asked.

'All right! Let's first examine what this wooden table is made of the way you would do it inside the cave. It essentially contains molecules that comprise atoms. An atom consists of a nucleus that is surrounded by several negatively charged electrons. The nucleus of an atom contains protons, each with a positive charge, and neutrons, which are electrically neutral. Depending on how the presence of an electron is measured, it behaves either as a very small particle or as a "cloud" that orbits the nucleus. Interestingly, protons and neutrons are not solid either. They are made up of other particle-like phenomena, so-called quarks. However, when it comes to answering your question, here is what really matters.'

Some in the group looked confused.

'What matters is the actual space that these particles occupy.'

'You mean their size?'

'Indeed! We would expect molecules to be tightly packed together to give us a sense of solidness but nothing is less true. However tightly packed molecules may be, they are made up of smaller atoms that almost entirely consist of empty space. The nucleus of an atom is about 100,000 times smaller than the atom itself. So if you'd put a nucleus, the size of a tennis ball, in the middle of a football stadium, the stadium perimeter would represent the boundary of an atom. Electrons, each much smaller than a nucleus, would orbit the tennis ball somewhere within the stadium boundaries.

'What you are effectively saying is that, at these subatomic levels, our world essentially consists of empty space!'

'That's right! Inside this wooden table, you'd find a subatomic abyss, a vast void that resembles outer space. Of course, the hand that knocks on the wooden table is no different.'

'Then, what explains our experience of solidness?' Abigail asked.

'When your hand touches the table, abundantly repeated behavior patterns, both of nuclei and electrons, are on a collision course. So behavior patterns not only sustain the space occupied by atoms but, in the process, they also produce the solidness that we experience.'

'If we explore this on ever smaller scales wouldn't we eventually get to an ultimate thing or actor rather than a behavior pattern?'

'I am afraid that is not the consensus in science. At the smallest possible length, at so-called Max Planck lengths, 16 times a billionth of a billionth of a billionth of a billionth meter, you'd probably see closed vibrating strings, not unlike elastic bands, that make up fundamental particles such as electrons and quarks. The essence of these strings is pure motion. So, even on exceptionally small scales, existence outside the cave involves behavior patterns, motion and memory.'

'I don't understand the memory bit,' Phil said.

'Repetition! Repeatedly vibrating behavior patterns are memories or reflections of inequalities that emerged earlier!'

'Of course, *the stroll*! That's what the *path of Emzine* is about,' Phil mumbled relieved.

'How does the worldview outside the cave serve us more than what we know in the back of the cave?' Abigail asked.

'The worldview in the back of the cave serves us fine when we measure or explain matters within a certain environment, context or timeframe. To explain biochemical phenomena, for example, we rest on rules that apply in biochemistry. When it comes to matters of physics or society, other rules apply. So, to interpret the world around us, we need to rely on experts that have specialized in a specific field.'

'That isn't necessarily bad, is it?'

'No, it isn't! Yet, it prevents us from grasping our world as a whole, from developing a more holistic view of paths of least resistance. The world of behavior patterns, on the other hand, pertains across fields. Whereas the language may be different in each field, the grammar or path of emergence applies regardless of the actors and context. The grammar of emergence is universal. As a result, it will now be much easier to assess how phenomena in the different fields relate to one another when searching for paths of least resistance.'

'Why is that so?'

'No matter whether we deal with human organizations, neural networks, phase transitions from liquid to gas or the inflation of the universe, we can now compare apples to apples essentially because, as behavioral marvels, all phenomena share the same four universal stages of emergence, of which the basic characteristics are known. As a result, we may now cross much broader rivers by lining up phenomena in other fields as steppingstones towards novel paths of least resistance.'

'How do you mean that?'

'When, for example, an organization traverses a certain stage of its emergence, it may benefit from the effect of phenomena in different fields that pass through the same or another stage of emergence. This is an example of advanced stage specialization.'

'How should I imagine this?'

'For example, a company may link up with customer and supplier organizations that are in the same stage of development and think the same way. A company may cross broad downstream rivers by using client and supplier companies as steppingstones, as it were.'

'Of course.'

'Alternatively, by working with organizations that are in another stage of development, a company may pull itself up by the bootstraps of another company. For example, a company that is entirely focused on bringing products to the market may seek to work with companies that traverse another stage of development to attract the necessary product and process innovations.'

Gabi, who had followed the discussion with interest, stirred in his chair.

'This reminds me of what they call "gauge theory" in physics,' he said.

'Would you mind filling us in on this, Gabi?' M said.

'As the term "gauge" suggests, gauge theory involves consistency of *measurement*. In other words, it signals whether a theory applies when the conditions change. Theories are said to have either *global* or *local symmetry*.'

'What do they mean by symmetry?' Phil asked.

'Well, symmetry refers to the symmetry between the answers that a theory produces. Theories are said to have *global symmetry* when they produce similar answers *across a broad range of conditions* or *globally*. Theories are said to have *local symmetry* when they produce similar answers *only when the local conditions are exactly the same*.'

'From what I gathered so far, outside the cave, the *path of Emzine* and its four stages of emergence have *global symmetry* because, no matter what the conditions or actors, the *path of Emzine* applies. On the other hand, in the back of the cave, matters line up only when the conditions compare. In other words, the theories of the prisoners in the back of the cave have *local symmetry*,' Gaby said.

'Can you illustrate this through an example?' Phil asked.

'Outside the cave, no matter what the actors or conditions, all forms of organization consistently traverse the same four stages of congruent-simultaneity or behavior-pattern emergence. However, inside the cave, the time that these organizations take to cycle through these stages differs generally. Only when the actors and local conditions are *exactly* the same, do the duration of phenomena inside the cave compare.'

'Does this bear any relation with the way "time" is measured in the back of the cave and outside the cave?' Eve asked.

'What is behind your question, Eve?' Phil interjected.

'Well, in the back of the cave, the prisoners rely on historical time or *Time Small*. Remember, the ancient Egyptians referred to it as "a dream that passes." Outside the cave, escapees measure *Time Great*—that is, the four stages of *congruent-simultaneity* emergence that are "endless in the cosmic life."' Eve said.

'So what?'

'Well, could it be that local-symmetry theories involve *Time Small* or *historical time* while global-symmetry theories rely on *Time Great* or *congruent-simultaneity emergence?*'

'I would think so,' Gabi said pensively. 'For one, Einstein's theory of relativity suggests that even the measurement of historical time or *Time Small* is dependent on local conditions. For example, to an observer on Earth, the time inside a space ship that travels near the speed of light will seem to have slowed down.

'Hmm, I see.'

'On the other hand, the laws of thermodynamics, which are at the heart of the *path of Emzine*, are valid no matter what the conditions or actors.'

'All this means that we, as escapees, will become futurists rather than historians,' Chandra noted.

'Why is that?' Phil asked

'In the back of the cave, away from the world of behavior-pattern emergence outside the cave, the prisoners are confined to sequential analyses when describing how a situation might change from one state to another. Inspired by historical trends, they'll produce, at best, projections of what might happen in the immediate future.'

'Okay, go on!' Phil said encouragingly.

'Through the *path of Emzine*, escapees see a much broader picture of how events interrelate with one another and how they will unfold in the future. They'll be able to see several stages ahead and prepare for the era or time when these stages emerge. As a result, they will not only be able to improve their choice of measures but also minimize the pain incurred.'

'What "pain" are you referring to?' Abigail asked

'Some of today's national leaders are inclined to preserve the present state no matter what because they assume that our world develops in a linear way. However, when a nation is not allowed to follow its natural path of development, it will deteriorate to an extent that the wellbeing of a people is impaired,' Chandra said, surprised by her own intervention.

'Will you be able to identify *when* future events occur?' Abigail asked

'You'll be able to identify which future stages of development will occur but not necessarily when. Then again, because you know what signals to look out for, you'll be well positioned to read the early signals of transitions that are about to emerge.'

M smiled as he watched the interaction unfolding. The group was rising to the occasion.

'We should indeed explore how the *path of Emzine* will change the relationship between organization and leader sometime!'

Then he slowly turned to Gabi.

'May I ask what brought you here?'

Gabi smiled shyly and took some time to compose himself. He was clearly not used to being at the center of attention.

'It occurred to me that a number of fairly recent scientific insights, each seemingly standing on itself, might well be related much more than we currently realize. What seems to be missing is an underlying "ontology" that brings these insights together conceptually. So I am searching for a new insight or philosophy, an integrative platform, as it were, that will help us further open a door that appears to be ajar, a door to a novel world of interpretation and even a new science.'

M nodded in understandment.

'Forgive me for interrupting,' Phil said, 'but what do you mean exactly by "ontology?"'

'Sorry, Phil! By "ontology," I mean an "explanation of existence." So I am searching for a new view of existence that will help us open the gate to new interpretations...'

'...and to new opportunities, of course!' Phil added.

'Yes, particularly those! Why else would I search for something?' Gabi responded with a broad smile.

'What turns something into a platform?' Phil asked

'An explanation or theory, such as the *path of Emzine*, offers principles that function as *foundational pillars of explanation* across the different sciences. This means you can build on it!'

'Then what is an *integrative* platform?'

'The *path of Emzine* explains all phenomena of existence as emergent behavior patterns. It allows you to associate diverse forms of existence and thus compare apples to apples whatever the actors involved.'

'Did you find in the *path of Emzine* what you were looking for?' she asked.

'Well, I think so! In my opinion, the *path of Emzine* represents a complementary explanation of existence, if not a theory of existence, that provides oxygen to the explanation of several natural phenomena that have either been observed or presumed.'

'Why complementary?' Phil persisted.

'The *path of Emzine* doesn't necessarily replace other explanations of existence but adds to them! To use your much-used parable, it adds to traditional explanations of existence just as the experience outside the cave adds to the experience inside the cave.'

'Thanks a lot, Gabi!' Phil said, indicating that she finally understood his rationale.

'You're welcome!'

'I'd be very interested to know which recent scientific insights you have in mind,' M said.

'Hmm, let me see.

'Inspired by the work of the Dutch theoretical physicist, Hendrik Casimir, quantum mechanics, a branch of physics that describes the interaction between subatomic particles, predicts that in very small and completely empty spaces [sometimes referred to as absolute vacuum], particles and their opposites, so-called antiparticles, may spontaneously emerge to annihilate each other thereafter.'

Gabi paused for a moment.

'Although all traces of matter are missing from these exceptionally small spaces, they contain energy fields. This is why quantum mechanics suggests that subatomic particles may arise from this nothingness when energy waves add up, as it were.'

'Nothing wrong with that, right?' Eve observed.

'Well, it reminds me of the prisoners in the back of the cave. Their theories may be accurate when predicting what might be observed in the back of the cave—that is, *locally*—but they leave the question of what takes place *globally* unanswered, such as the relationship with other behavioral phenomena.'

'So this leads you to the domain outside the cave?"

'Indeed! The spontaneous emergence of observable matter is more plausible and more explicable, in a world that is believed to consist of behavior patterns. For one, empty space will obviously be populated by behavior patterns because it represents an inequality or niche that needs to be minimized. During the minimizing process, particles become visible during one stage of emergence when least-energy fitting behavior patterns reproduce. These visible phenomena disappear again in the stage that follows.'

'Of course, this is a fairly sketchy example,' Abigail interjected.

'Which will become less and less sketchy as I add other examples,' Gabi responded, not in the least deterred.

'Why?'

'A string of examples becomes a pattern!'

Abigail smiled and gestured in a capitulating manner.

'My next example involves the rather common confusion about the nature of time. To us, time appears to move *forward*—that is, from the past to the future—and not backward. For example, when you melt an ice cube, the resulting pool of water will not form an ice cube by itself again if you lower the temperature. Neither would you see a lump of sugar reassemble itself after you dissolve it in a cup of tea. In other words, time forward is *not* the same as time backward and, thus, time is not reversible.

'However, at subatomic levels where the predictions of physicists are dictated by the possibility or chance of events occurring, events may flow both forward and backward in time. Physicists call this "time symmetry" because, at these levels, you can, in theory, undo something simply by reversing the process calculations.'

'In my humble view, it's hard to believe that a star will reassemble itself after it explodes,' Umberto said.

'Indeed! On cosmic scales, time does not appear to be reversible. So, confined by laws of quantum mechanics that have been shown to predict subatomic events quite accurately, physicists now ponder why the "symmetry of time" at subatomic levels is "broken" at cosmic levels.'

'Why?' Eve asked.

'Well, assuming that the universe evolved from subatomic scales to its current size, physicists wonder when and, for what reasons, the reversibility of time was lost.'

'Hmm, I see!'

'Strangely enough, physicists agree on the reasons why time is *not* reversible *now*!'

'Why is that?'

'As the universe expands, energy is converted from one form into another at the cost of energy that is wasted, a form of energy that can no longer be used.'

'Aha, you mean *entropy*!'

'That's right. Because energy is wasted as entropy, you cannot reverse a process because you lost some of the energy that you started off with.'

'So, how does the *path of Emzine* provide clarity here?'

'The worlds inside and outside the cave offer two notions of time that might help resolve the confusion about the *arrow of time.* In my view, the idea of time as a sequential or chronological measure, which is either reversible or non-reversible, is a back-in-the-cave perception of time that lacks an outside-the-cave perspective. Of course, outside the cave, the four stages of congruent-simultaneity development tell you what "time" it *really* is!'

'So?'

'Well, the definition of time at subatomic levels might need to be refined based on the worldview outside the cave.'

'What makes you believe this is possible?' Umberto asked.

'A little-known paper by the Russian theoretical physicist, Eugene Maslov.' [5]

'May I ask what it is about?'

'Maslov explores a universal description of the transition of matter, such as the transition from gas to liquid, when no any energy is wasted.'

'Aha, do you mean that no entropy is generated?'

'That's right! Of course, when no energy is wasted or no entropy is produced, time might be reversible.'

'Of course! Remarkable!' Umberto mumbled.

'Wait until you hear this! By minimizing the energy wasted and by focusing entirely on the dynamics of transitions where one form of matter gradually replaces another, Maslov neatly arrived at four stages that resemble the four stages of congruent-simultaneity emergence. Moreover, like the four-stage cycles of behavior-pattern development, Maslov's cycle of four stages also leads to the next cycle through a stage of "turbulence" or chaos. Hence, these cycles might be "endless in the cosmic life."'

'Which transitions of matter did Maslov have in mind exactly?'

'Inspired by his collaboration with a scientist of the Russian Institute of Metal Physics, Maslov referred to transitions from gas to liquid and

---

[5] *Parametric Resonance As Possible Cause Of Spontaneous Transition From Meta-stable States,* Annales de la Fondation Louis de Broglie, Vol. 26 Spécial, 2001

from liquid to solid, as well as to the displacement of atoms in a crystal, the distortion in shape-memory alloys, and so on.'

'That doesn't deal with the definition of time at subatomic levels.'

'The thought also occurred to Maslov which is why he illustrated the parallels with transitions at subatomic levels. Interestingly, he noted that these stages could even be proven "to give rise to a stationary [subatomic] foam-like spatial structure that could manifest itself as the cellular structure of the universe" at large!'

'This suggests that the definition of *time outside the cave* is valid at cosmic as well as subatomic levels,' Umberto said pensively.

'That's right. Now, you can imagine why I believe that the *path of Emzine* might function as an integrative platform.'

Umberto nodded enthusiastically.

'You probably have more examples,' M said.

Gabi nodded.

'As you discussed at length, behavior patterns that convert energy to minimize local inequalities are behind the universe that we observe. In the end, when the entropy that is produced in the process reaches a certain level, the universe will literally be short of the behavior patterns needed to sustain its spatial magnitude. As a result, it will collapse. Consequently, in order for entropy to increase on *the path of Emzine*, it must have been low at the beginning of our universe, and other infant universes, where that was not the case, must have been doomed to disappear.'

'How exactly is this supported by actual findings?' Umberto asked.

'Well, the research of the theoretical physicist and cosmologist, Laura Mersini-Houghton, and her distinguished colleagues[6] indeed suggests that multiple infant universes must have emerged and that only the low-entropy version(s) survived.'

Umberto appeared to be impressed by the evidence so far.

'I have four more examples that push the ripples of the *path of Emzine* to ever-broader circles of science. Three of these illustrate how the

---

[6] http://uk.arxiv.org/PS_cache/arxiv/pdf/0809/0809.3623v1.pdf

behavioral perspective of our world is capturing the minds of prominent scientists.'

It was clear that Gabi now had everyone's undivided attention.

'One example concerns the global effort to identify gravity as one of Nature's four basic force fields. Einstein himself helped kick this off. So far, in spite of mind-boggling conjectures, involving string theory, this research has been fruitless.

'Recently, the Dutch theoretical physicist and string-theorist, Erik Verlinde, surprised his colleagues by an article, in which he argued that gravity is not one of Nature's basic forces but, rather, an *emergent* or *entropic* force. He later uttered that other so-called fundamental forces might not be fundamental either.'[7]

'Please, remind me of the meaning of entropic force again?' Phil interjected.

'Remember the example of the two connected containers at OYO where the motion of the more vigorous molecules in one container made them move to the other container?

'Well, the force that makes these molecules move is called an entropic force because it increases entropy by spreading the colliding behavior of molecules while establishing equilibrium across the two containers. Briefly, entropic force is at the heart of the world of behavior patterns outside the cave and, thus, at the heart of the *path of Emzine*. This is essentially why the findings of Verlinde seem to support the behavioral view of our world.'

'Of course!' Phil murmured.

'To test the idea of gravity as entropic force, Verlinde studied the behavior of molecules inside an elastic band. When you stretch an elastic band, you feel the force that wants to bring it back to its original shape at which it is in equilibrium.

'Let us briefly return to the dialogue at OYO again. When equilibrium was reestablished between the two connected containers, the entropy increased. Likewise, when you let an elastic band snap back to its original shape, entropy is produced as spin-off. That's why the force that

---

[7] http://arxiv.org/pdf/1001.0785

tries to bring the elastic band to its original state of equilibrium is called an entropic force.

'When it comes to gravity, the story is no different. On the surface of the Earth, you are in a state of gravitational equilibrium. The moment you jump, you experience the same effect as when you stretch an elastic band—that is, you are drawn back to Earth by an entropic force until equilibrium has been reestablished.

'Eve once referred to entropy as the *cost of energy conversion*. As you might have guessed, Verlinde similarly defines gravity as "the cost of moving things around." Of course, when you move things around, energy is converted.'

Everyone was in sync, except Phil that is.

'I now understand the idea of *entropic force* but where does the expression "emergent force" come from?' she asked.

'Again, the *path of Emzine* provides conceptual guidance. When you bring something out of a state of equilibrium, you effectively create an inequality. Then, behavior patterns emerge to minimize the inequality as fast as the local circumstances allow. In the process, entropy is produced. Therefore, as behavior patterns emerge, so does *entropic force*.'

'Incidentally, the American physicist, Edwin Jaynes, brought the two terms together by stating that entropy is a "measure of reproducibility of process." Of course, on the *path of Emzine*, behavior patterns reproduce abundantly. Hence, "reproduction" signals "entropy production" as well as "emergence."' M added.

'The idea that our world gets meaning through behavior patterns is crucial,' Gabi continued. 'This leads me to another example, which shows that *motion* holds evidence of reproducing behavior patterns not detectable to the naked eye. The Italian-French mathematician, Joseph-Louis Lagrange, managed to lay bare *the invisible outlines of paths of least resistance of reproducing behavior patterns*, such as the outlines of currents in the sea. These so-called "Lagrangian coherent structures" can only be made visible through complex computational tools. Not surprisingly, coherent structures show up across a broad range of phenomena no matter what the actors involved, from the movement of a crowd inside a railway station to the movement of molecules in the ocean. What is more important, they also help predict future events.'

'Wow! Didn't expect this!' Zander whispered to Abigail.

'My next example arises from another branch of science: *biology*. DNA is generally considered to be the database or code of life. It is a complex molecule that consists of two long and twisted sequences of chemical substances that are connected by horizontal bars not unlike the steps of a ladder. In humans, these sequences have about 25,000 segments or "units of inheritance" called *genes*.

'The DNA-code plays a crucial role as the blueprint when cells reproduce. This explains why the structure of DNA must be stable. It is assumed to change by chance only, for example, as a result of cell-division errors.

'It is remarkable that this explanation survived "unchanged" as long as it did!'

'Why?' Eve asked, surprised.

'Well, according to this explanation, inequalities emerging in the environment would leave the DNA-code largely untouched.'

'That is strange, indeed! You wonder how living creatures would adapt to changing environments other than through accidental cell-division errors. Of course, this would make the *path of Emzine* useless as a beacon of guidance,' Eve offered.

'That's right! Fortunately, a more subtle explanation surfaced in the mean time which hinges on the behavioral nature of our world.'

'You make me really curious now,' Eve said.

'The 73-year-old Swedish scientist, Lars Olov Bygren, studied the effect of feast and famine winters in very cold, isolated and sparsely populated areas that conveniently served as reaction tubes.[8] Bygren's research revealed that the offspring of kids, who went from normal eating to overeating in rare warm and, thus, overabundant winters, produced offspring that died six years earlier on average. In line with the *path of Emzine*, I might add, the research of Bygren demonstrated the

---

[8] *Longevity Determined*, Acta Biotheoretica, 2001, Volume 49, Number 1

link between temperature inequality, behavior patterns and the health of offspring, which evidently depends on DNA. However, assuming that the DNA-code remained unchanged, which it did, the question was how this could have happened.'

'I don't understand why people die earlier when eating richly,' Phil asked.

'Separate research showed that mammals, that live on the edge of starvation, live longer than those that eat abundantly. This explains why overweight people tend to live shorter.'

'Hmm, I see.'

'The findings of Bygren led to the suspicion that the temperature-inspired change of eating behaviors had either switched on or off certain DNA-code segments.

'It turned out that this is common practice inside the human body. Because all cell types contain the same DNA, *local* inequalities either silence or activate sequences of DNA to help cells differentiate and grow into skin cells, organ cells, and so on.'

'How should I imagine this?' Eve asked.

'Just outside the DNA molecule, chemicals above the ladder of sequences—that is, the ladder seen on its side—function as "flags" that turn genes on or off. These chemicals are called the "epigenome," the prefix, *epi,* meaning *above.* The science that emerged from these findings is fittingly named "epigenetics." To me, this is another example of how the behavioral view of our world is gradually being embraced.'

'Overwhelmingly so!' Umberto observed.

'I find it hard to accept that DNA changes by chance only!' Phil said.

'Why?' Eve asked.

'Well, what produces cell-division errors, do you think?'

'A waterfall of local and global inequalities,' Eve said.

'Well, there you go!' Phil reacted.

'You are quite right, Phil!' Gabi said.

'Your observation brings me to my next example, which is centered on Nature's primary search for paths of least resistance or, more precisely, Nature's search for congruent-simultaneity opportunities.'

'Tell me more!' Phil said.

'Well, one might say that the "affection for congruent simultaneity" is the primordial miracle that rules our world and its emergence. Considering that matters of energy efficiency are behind this miracle, my point is that Nature, not unlike water that flows downhill, is inclined to tread similar paths and arrive at common solutions.'

'So?' Abigail asked eagerly.

'Well, the tendency to arrive at common solutions is at the heart of the conjecture of the Cambridge University academic, Simon Conway Morris, who specializes in evolutionary paleobiology.'

'Evolutionary paleobiology?' Phil asked.

'The prefix, *paleo*, refers to matters related to the geological past. So Conway Morris explores the emergence of biological phenomena going very far back in history.'

'Okay, thanks!'

'In his book, *Life's Solution*, Conway Morris identifies numerous examples where Nature arrives at common solutions whenever a new branch emerged on the tree of species and, indeed, regardless of the direction that history took.[9] In excessive detail, Conway Morris shows how Nature's solutions "converge" to common traits that we observe in, say, mammals today, such as two eyes, four "legs," one mouth closely positioned near the brain, high oxygen-carrying capacity of the blood, a single aorta, seven neck vertebrae, and so on.'

'Does this also apply to societal solutions?' Chandra asked.

'Societal or behavioral solutions also appear to converge and echo throughout history, which might explain why leaders today are still inspired by the tactics of an ancient Chinese warrior and why history seems to repeat itself.'

'Doesn't this prove the hand of God?' Abigail asked hesitantly.

'For the biased mind, including Conway Morris's, it might, at least on first sight. This becomes apparent in the last few chapters of his book, where he unwraps his thus-far hidden agenda.'

'Why do you believe he is biased? Abigail interjected.

---

[9] *Life's Solution*, Cambridge University Press, 2003

'Not only is Cambridge University a Christian bastion of academic endeavor, but Conway Morris's links with the Templeton Foundation also indicate that his agenda is at least in part ruled by the desire to marry the charter of science to the charter of religion. Of course, that does not in any way diminish his formidable findings.'

'Interesting, to say the least!' Umberto muttered.

'Conway Morris's primary aim was to disprove Darwin's idea that evolution is blindly driven by chance only, an idea that was staunchly defended by a remarkable and renowned colleague, the late American paleontologist, Stephen Jay Gould. Mind you, if ruled by chance, Nature might arrive at different and diverging solutions each time. In my view, Conway Morris convincingly shows that chance, as the alleged principle behind evolution, fails to explain the substantial evidence of *convergent solutions* and *adaptation*. Yet, at the same time, he misses an opportunity to suggest an alternative rule. Instead, he mistakenly puts the door ajar to a religious perspective.'

'Why mistakenly?' Abigail asked.

'Surprisingly, Conway Morris doesn't show his usual rigor when it comes to claims that hint at the religious dimension. In the end, he tries to rescue his torn image when he notes: "*None of it presupposes, let alone proves the existence of God, but all is congruent.*" However, by that time, the damage was done.'

'So, how does Conway Morris's research support the behavioral perspective of our world and the *path of Emzine*?' Abigail asked.

'In harmony with Conway Morris' evidence, the *path of Emzine* leads our world of behavior-pattern species, not unlike a river, to familiar paths of least resistance no matter what the initial conditions.'

'I don't get this. My understanding is that minutely different initial conditions determine the behavior of natural systems,' Umberto said.

'Initial conditions determine the paths that rivers follow locally. At a global level, however, their paths persistently lead down to the sea. Don't forget, on the *path of Emzine*, Nature *blindly* pursues congruent simultaneity through paths of least resistance.'

'I see what you mean!'

'Of course, a world of behavior patterns is not just more adaptive. It *is* a world of adaptation. When inequalities arise in the environment, behavior-pattern species spontaneously emerge and cascade. On the whole, the findings of Conway Morris support the *path of Emzine* as much as the *path of Emzine* explains Conway Morris's findings.'

Gabi looked at M, confident that he had made his case.

'Thank you, Gabi!' I am most impressed by your analyses, which, indeed, solidly strengthen the premise of the world outside the cave. Initially, you referred to the need for an integrative platform of philosophy and to the need for a new science. Your examples leave little doubt about the *path of Emzine* as an explanation of existence that gives new meaning to today's scientific findings. The question is whether it also hints at the need for a new science,' M said.

In a silent corner of the room, Abdul waved a hand.

M turned to him and encouraged him to speak.

'I am truly inspired by what I have heard so far. Your question about the need for a new science also intrigues me. Let me explain briefly why this is so. My name is Abdul. I am a Muslim by birth *and* a scientist. From a very early age, I have been fascinated by how a scientific perspective might help us discover the principles that rule our world, other than those that have been expounded in the Koran by our holy Prophet. I studied the history of Islamic science and became enlightened by the work of *Ibn Rushd* or, in Latin, *Averroes*. Born in 1126 in Córdoba, Averroes is one of the most prominent polymaths that the Islamic culture has ever produced. He is generally viewed as the founding father of secular thought in Western Europe and has influenced the work of Western thinkers, such as René Descartes and Moses Maimonides.'

'Sorry to interrupt but what is a "polymath" and what do you mean by "secular"?' Phil asked.

'A *polymath* is someone that has an exceptionally broad command of several fields of knowledge. Averroes, for example, specialized in Aristotelian philosophy, Islamic philosophy, Islamic law, logic, psychology, politics, Arabian music, medicine, astronomy, geography, mathematics, physics and celestial mechanics; I mean, the calculation of the paths of heavenly bodies in the sky. *Secular thought* refers to a separation of science from religion or of the state from religion, as is currently the situation in Turkey, for example.'

'I see, thanks!'

'Averroes is particularly known for his treatise "The Incoherence of the Incoherence" or "The Unintelligibility of the Unintelligibility" in which he argues that the rational philosophy of Aristotle fits rather than fights Islamic thinking. Writing in dialogue form, not unlike Plato did, Averroes attempts to create harmony between philosophy and faith. His ideas were very successful in Europe but, unfortunately, ill received by contemporary Islamic scholars.'

Abdul paused before making his final pitch.

'I set myself the goal to continue and expand the work of Averroes starting with a simple question. If the Koran expounds the rule of Allah to the followers of Islam then how do other forms of existence that cannot read or memorize his texts apply his rule?'

Abdul briefly hesitated.

'To be frank, I am in part motivated to pursue this road because I fear that the way pieces of the Koran are sometimes driven down the throat of young unassuming followers may produce unintended side effects that the Prophet might have regretted had he lived today. Moreover, the rigor with which followers cite the Koran may reinforce their sense of *being* in the face of Allah but not necessarily their sense of *becoming*. I guess, the same holds for other religions.'

'Make sure to be very prudent because you'll be walking on a tightrope in the sky! The "side effects" that you refer to may shake the rope until you fall and...'

'Die?' Abdul finished M's sentence. 'I am well aware of this. That's why I shall keep both the interest and interests of God-fearing Islamic followers upfront in my mind. Of course, as a scientist I realize too well that the *path of Emzine* may indeed represent Allah's rule.'

'Keep in mind, the *path of Emzine* may not just be "Allah's rule" but also even be Allah!'

'However much that inference stretches my Islamic mind the thought occurred to me too. That's why I think it is essential first to see what this new science produces. Once its findings have rooted in society, I'll look at my options again. Time is on my side.'

The personal mission of Abdul and his willingness to re-explore the foundations of his faith visibly impressed everyone in the group, not in the least Zander.

'You inspire me Abdul!' Zander said.

'A Moslem inspiring a Christian?' Abdul responded with a smile.

'Didn't the medieval priest, Thomas Aquinas, feed on Averroes's analysis of Aristotle's philosophy too?' Zander replied.

'The inspiration that is required now should go much deeper than the selective plum picking by Aquinas. Remember, it is not the interest of a religion that is at stake but the foundations of our world, foundations that will identify religion as an emergent marvel too,' Eve said.

'As a temporary phenomenon, you mean?' Abigail asked terrified.

'Yes, that is what Eve means to say,' Zander whispered to her.

'So, what should be at the heart of this new science? What would it entail?' M said.

'So far, all our discussions were centered on the emergence of a broad range of phenomena. So it must be a science that explores, explains and classifies examples of *emergence*,' Eve offered.

'Aren't the regular sciences doing that?' Abigail asked.

'They do to a certain extent but they don't look at the parallels as the *path of Emzine* does nor do they look at "emergence" per se.'

'I'd say, it should be the *science of emergence*, a meta-science that deals with phenomena of emergence across the sciences,' Umberto said.

'What do you mean by meta-science?' Phil asked.

'With the prefix, *meta*, I mean to say that the science of emergence goes *across* the sciences. The Greek word, *meta*, means "across."'

'How does a meta-science distinguish itself?'

'Well, whereas traditional sciences search for consistencies within a particular field, a meta-science searches for consistencies across fields.

In my opinion, a meta-science should particularly also study how effects specific to certain sciences might re-enforce effects in other sciences.'

'Considering the discussion at OYO, the *science of emergence* should be rooted in thermodynamics and chaos theory. These should be its anchors, as it were,' Gabi advised.

'Why chaos theory again?' Phil asked.

'Chaos theory explains the interaction between actors, no matter what they are. Remember?'

'What would academics that specialize in the science of emergence *do*? Phil asked, surprised by her own persistence.

'I'd suggest that they'd study the similarities and differences between phenomena of emergence across the sciences in the different stages of emergence focusing on thermodynamic matters, chaos-theory-related matters, and behavioral matters.'

'Of course I am playing the devil's advocate but what would be the use of the science of emergence? What would we gain from it?'

'It would help us achieve a better and hands-on understanding of the *path of Emzine*,' Gabi said

'So what?'

'Don't forget, a better understanding of the *path of Emzine* also means a better understanding of the purpose of humankind. It would help us identify who and what we really are!'

'Hmm, I see! Any other gains?'

'Because energy efficiency is at the heart of the *path of Emzine*, you are likely to see breakthrough improvements in how we manage our world. Because all events develop following the same four stages of emergence, we'd know what would be ahead of us. Together with our growing intelligence of what makes things tick in these stages, we'd be so much better prepared to deal with the future.'

'Considering our newfound perspective of the world outside the cave, I wouldn't be surprised if the science of emergence would also help us revisit and refine the moral grounds of society,' Eve added.

Phil seemed content, for the moment.

'I realize that we haven't adequately evaluated the effect of the *path of Emzine* on science yet but, at least, we have identified "a vehicle" in the shape of the *science of emergence* that may help us tackle this challenge in the future,' M said.

'Anyhow, we should call it a day as it is getting late. As usual, we have covered a great deal. What do you think?'

The group, as a whole, spontaneously turned to Gabi and Abdul choosing them as spokesmen for the occasion. It was Gabi who opted to share his thoughts first.

'I learned more than I could have imagined when I made the odd decision to join this session. We literally bodily explored the *path of Emzine* during our Noordhoek stroll. We tested its relevance regarding physical realities, even getting down to levels where "string theorists" normally wander. I am grateful for your collective help in ordering my thoughts as to the transformation in thinking that is silently unfolding in the world of science. On the whole, I gather, this session bridged the philosophical and the practical. Of course, many questions need to be asked still and, then, of course, we face the challenge of effectively establishing a science of emergence.'

'I second that. This session and the interaction with all of you gave wings to my aims and hopes. I am intrigued by the possibility of fine-tuning our moral grounds. Indeed, what and when is something immoral? Why are acts of immorality committed anyway? What are the mechanisms that are at work and how can and should we deal with these? Also, how will our understanding of the *path of Emzine* affect economics? More questions than I can list at this point! In short, I'd like to explore the effect of the *path of Emzine* on the social sciences.'

Those that looked around when Gabi and Abdul spoke would have noticed expressions of sincere empathy. They might also have noticed the remaining doubts that still lingered in the minds of some. The group soon dispersed after plans for the next session were discussed. M looked relaxed, apparently in anticipation of the scenery on the way back.

Toward A More Predictable World

Once a cattle post established by Dutch soldiers in 1672, Somerset West is situated on the slopes of the Hottentot-Holland Mountains facing the False Bay shores in the South. To get to these mountains, coming from Stellenbosch, you'd turn left into Lourensford Road on Main Street close to the town center. Lourensford Road leads to the entrance of the 10,000-acre Lourensford Estate, named after the river that originates there. It takes a day to explore this immense estate by utility vehicle. The return on investment comes in stunning views of a bare mountain ridge that is lavishly laced with exceptionally lush foothills.

Phil planned a picnic for the group on the estate in between two wine fields ten minutes by bus from the restaurant at the entrance. At this unusual venue, the estate's staff had arranged a nicely dressed table and some umbrellas that provided the shade needed for a comfortable get-together. The group was brought to the venue by a Golden Arrow bus, the same bus that brought farmworkers to the fields that morning. Once at the location, some started scouting the immediate environment. Others took a seat at one of the tables and watched the magnificent view.

M was the first to see the cloud of dust produced by a large black car that was approaching fast. Someone stepped out and the car drove off. M soon recognized the person walking in their direction.

'That must be Charlene,' he whispered to himself.

M had met Charlene some years ago at a conference in the north of the country where he had appeared as one of the speakers. Born on the Cape Flats, a violent township area near Cape Town, Charlene had worked her way through high school to earn her bachelor's and master's degrees from Cape Town University. Then she managed to secure the scholarships needed also to earn a master's *and* a doctorate from Harvard University. When M first met Charlene, she was an established director of one of South Africa's banks and a professor in Human Resource Management. Having heard about M's speech on the emergence of organization and leadership, Charlene became intrigued by the singular views that M had presented. M was pleased that Charlene had offered to join the dialogue during a recent telephone conversation. Unassuming, friendly, but razor-sharp if need be, Charlene would be an essential contributor to the session that was to come.

M greeted Charlene warmly, after which he introduced her to his newfound friends.

Phil made sure that everyone was properly seated and, then, kicked of the session.

'Welcome everyone! Welcome to this remarkable location which I happened to find by chance. By chance? Well, I was looking for a place of inspiration close to Nature to continue our dialogue. That might explain why my eyes settled here.'

Murmurs of agreement arose from the group.

'Did you know that leopards have been spotted here? Apparently, they are reproducing sufficiently again in what was once their habitat.'

Some in the group started to look uneasy.

'Don't worry! They told me that leopards avoid people. By the way, they generally hunt during the night and typically wander in the mountains over there.'

Phil pointed to the massive mountain ridge that seemed *so* close but, in reality, was much further away than the naked eye would admit.

'Leopards are solitary hunters; I learned that their survival is in part due to their behavioral adaptability. In view of our previous discussions, isn't that interesting?' Eve contributed.

A wave of recognition travelled through the group.

'Leopards are on their own but what changes when animals operate in groups?' M asked.

'You mean like lions, for example?' Eve asked.

'Indeed, like lions!'

'Well, compared to other cats, lions are exceptionally social. A pride of lions typically includes some related females and their offspring as well as a male or an alliance of a few males. Increased hunting success is assumed to be the benefit of a pride. In answer to your question, each member of the pride fulfills a specific role. The lionesses mainly hunt. The males look after the territorial interests of the pride. Yet, when the pride needs to be defended, both males and females come into action.'

'Because *roles* are involved, the *path of Emzine* also explains a pride of lions, right?' Phil asked.

Eve gestured affirmatively.

'Have you ever watched a group of lions hunting?' M asked.

Eve nodded and so did some others in the group.

'What did you notice?'

'Well, the group moves in what seems to be a coordinated manner, almost as if they have a strategy. However, I discovered that, despite the encircling tactics, the group simply waits for their prey to come too close or wander off too far from the herd.'

'They wait for a big enough "inequality" to emerge, in other words.'

Eve nodded.

Some in the group were alerted by M's observation.

'What else?'

'Well, let me think. Hunting members of the pride consistently play certain roles in hunts.'

'Aha! Why do you think this is so?'

'Character, if not attitude...'

'Attitude?'

'I mean, each member of the hunting lot will do what he or she feels most comfortable with.'

'Do you mean like a *comfort zone*?'

'Indeed!'

'Comfort zones, such as?'

'Well, some take the initiative and explore the outskirts of a herd, at times walking straight through it. Others focus on making a kill. Yet others casually watch the reaction of the herd almost as if they are managing the dynamics of the group. Occasionally, you might see a lion disrupt the tactics followed and initiate an entirely different approach.'

'Yet, each of these cats acts as a leader in its own right,' M said.

'You might say so!' Eve responded.

'Did it ever occur to you that these *comfort zones* might be inspired by the four stages of behavior-pattern emergence?'

'Not really, but now I think of it, that would be kind of logical, right?'

'Considering that our world is entirely about least-energy fitting behavior patterns, it makes perfect sense for actors at the heart of these patterns to specialize in some way to accommodate the process.'

'True! These actors too involve least-energy fitting behavior patterns that must have once been triggered by inequalities,' Charlene offered.

M was visibly pleased that Charlene had decided to contribute this soon. She had prepared herself well for the occasion.

'Do you mean to say that actors are shaped by inequalities that occur in a certain stage of behavior-pattern emergence?' Eve asked.

'That is what my observations tell me,' Charlene said.

'So, actors should rise to the surface as leaders during a certain stage of development!'

'That is what should happen!'

'Should happen?'

'Leaders with the right comfort zone should ideally rise to the surface during a certain stage of behavior-pattern emergence and, sometimes, they do. Unfortunately, this is not always the case.'

'Why is this so?'

'Because society doesn't know yet about these matters, people often stumble into leadership positions because they happen to be around.

Then they are forced to take on a leadership role that doesn't fit their comfort zone and, as a result, an organization or nation is hampered in its development.'

'Hampered?'

'Well, when an organization or nation is not opting for the measures needed to traverse a certain stage of its development because a wrong-headed leader is in its way, it stalls.'

'Hmm, I see.'

'Of course, this leaves a largely unused opportunity to identify people or leaders whose natural comfort zone fits the needs of an evolving organization or nation,' Charlene added.

'How do people grow comfort zones, by the way? Phil asked.

'The process of comfort-zone development may well start before we are born when behavior patterns emerge and cascade in the fetus. Mind you, this doesn't just involve the brain but man's constitution of body and brain, the body giving meaning to the brain and the brain giving meaning to the body. Inequalities at all levels, from the biochemical to the behavioral, may determine the degree of "stage accommodation."'

'Stage accommodation?'

'Well, behavior patterns that emerge and cascade early in life are reflections of inequalities experienced in the predominant stage of development of the *local* environment *then*. So the cascades of behavior patterns that make up an individual are inspired by this stage.'

'So, one stage only?'

'Remnants of more stages may be found in each individual. However, behavior patterns of one particular stage tend to dominate as a result of the natural selection of the least-energy fitting. Of course, some comfort zones turn out to be more stage specific than others.'

'Does this mean that you can't change your comfort zone?'

'In theory, you can! For example, when part of the brain is destroyed, it can in some cases grow new neuron connections and then develop new cascades of neuron-cluster behavior. Again, the patterns involved will be inspired by the typical inequalities in the predominant stage of emergence of the local environment at the time.'

'So, we *can* change ourselves?'

'Unfortunately, under normal circumstances, when trying to change the way you interpret your world, you are competing with established cascades of neuron-cluster behavior patterns.'

'Competing?'

'Well, before and during such a process of change, you depend on the very cascades of neuron-cluster behavior that you hope to change. As a result, you'll almost inevitably spiral to a rathole of circular logic to end where you began.'

'I see! So what you are effectively saying is that you are what you are!' Phil said, disappointed by this newfound reality.

'Affirmative—that is, when it comes to individuals. However, this is not the case when it comes to organizations,' Charlene said.

'Why, may I ask?'

'Whereas it is exceptionally difficult to change established cascades of neuron-cluster behavior, it is quite possible to amend the cascades of behavior patterns inside an organization.'

'How?'

'Essentially, by changing the mix of leaders! For example, to facilitate an organization's progress to an imminent stage of its emergence, one should try to attract leaders with an "accommodating comfort zone" and rebalance its management teams. After all, leaders rely on their comfort zone when they assess the local and global environment and when they choose particular solutions. An "accommodating comfort zone" is one that satisfies the needs in an imminent stage of development.'

'Isn't that unfair to the people who contributed to the development of a company or organization so far?' Eve asked.

'On the contrary, the more a company or organization approaches the next stage of its development, the more these people become at odds with the changing corporate environment. Whereas they felt at one with the way "their" organization moved forward at first, they now become frustrated by issues that, to them, appear to have emerged out of nowhere. They also feel out of touch with the solutions suggested. As a result, they lose interest and may even start dragging their feet.'

'So, what do you do?'

'If you were aware of the actual stage of corporate or organizational development and of the comfort zone of the leaders involved, you might help these leaders transfer to an organization that traverses a stage of development where they are at their best. Of course, this would not just help these organizations but also increase the effectiveness and sense of achievement of these leaders.'

'This seems like a huge task,' Phil said.

'What do you mean?' Charlene asked.

'Well, transferring people that do not have the right comfort zone!'

'Don't get me wrong. I am only suggesting we tip the balance in favor of the comfort zone that lines up with an imminent stage of emergence. This means rotating some of the key opinion makers only. On the whole, organizations will continue to depend on all four comfort zones because parts of the organization as well as the supplier and client organizations are likely to traverse other stages of development. '

'What will this all produce in the end?' Eve asked.

'*Comfort-zone rebalancing* effectively increases the speed with which organizations traverse the various stages of their emergence because it helps them attract in good time the necessary leaders—that is, leaders who, due to their comfort zone, will facilitate the adoption of the most opportune stage-specific solutions. As a result, organizations will more rapidly reinvent themselves to return to a stage of growth generation.'

'That doesn't accord with my understanding of how consulting firms try to instill growth-generating capabilities. Consultants typically identify proven means of success to force feed these to their clients. If you'd inspire a company to traverse more rapidly through its stages of development instead, you would at some point steer it through a period of declining growth with the objective of creating an environment for renewal. Obviously, this is not necessarily something that a company would want to pay its consultants for.'

'I understand your reaction! The problem is that consulting firms typically follow a "Cartesian" approach, an approach that leads to success in specific cases only,' M said.

'Cartesian?' Phil interjected.

'The term "Cartesian" means an approach that is inspired by the work of René Descartes, a French mathematician and philosopher, who lived during the late Renaissance. In part inspired by mechanical dolls, that were fashionable then, Descartes arrived at a rather mechanistic view of our world. According to Descartes, our world and, thus, also organizations can be manipulated to improve their functioning—not unlike the mechanical contraptions of his time. However, as the *path of Emzine* shows, our world of behavioral patterns is ruled by fundamental laws that cannot tinkered with.'

'Are you saying that a Cartesian approach is based on inside-the-cave-thinking?'

'Exactly!'

'Then, what are companies paying consultants for?' Eve asked.

'Consultants play a crucial role in the transfer of measures, that have been shown to produce success, to companies on a path of growth. By cross-fertilizing the seeds of success from one company to another, they help companies reach their growth potential, as it were.'

'Nothing wrong with that, right?'

'That's right. However, consultants are powerless when they try to reinvigorate or stretch a company's growth-generating potential. Some consulting firms use recipes, abstractions of what they consider to be remedies, to push their clients into a straightjacket of success, almost as if they are dealing with psychiatric patients, but to no avail.'

'Why?'

'As I said, still treating organizations as "contraptions" rather than as phenomena of behavior-pattern emergence, many a consultant believes that an organization can be made to function better by fine-tuning its procedures and tweaking its dials. However, as studies by management scientists confirm, after a period of substantial growth, investments made to squeeze out even more growth are a waste of money. It's like beating a dead horse.'

'So, what *is* the right remedy?'

'Insofar as the use of "remedy" applies, it is to help organizations move on to the next stage of behavior-pattern development by comfort-zone rebalancing. When push comes to shove, comfort-zone rebalancing truly improves the "dexterity" of organizations and nations.'

'Dexterity meaning the skills to perform stage-specific and functional tasks, including reinventing an organization!' Eve noted.

M nodded and smiled when he realized that Eve referred to their first meeting at Hidden Valley.

'From what I gathered, a company may well disappear when the environmental conditions prevent it from reinventing itself. This means that companies cannot be built to last!' Umberto observed.

'That is correct. As phenomena of behavior-pattern emergence that arise to minimize certain inequalities in the market, companies can at best be grown to achieve and not really be built to last!' M concluded.

'Why is growth so important?' Abigail interjected.

'Growth simply is the only measure that shows whether successful behavior-pattern species out-reproduce other less effective ones.'

'Another benefit of comfort-zone rebalancing is a heightened sense of identity and becoming of the leaders involved,' Charlene added.

'Becoming? I remember you saying that we are what we are?' Eve noted.

'When it comes to our comfort zone, we are what we are. However, the comfort zone that grows in us when we emerge as individuals allows us to contribute to the emergence of our world. As such, we become as we help our world become. In other words, our role in the becoming of our world is what gives meaning to our existence.'

'Intriguing and inspiring!'

'It'll give us a sense of purpose too! As we discussed at Mount Nelson, we are Nature's most advanced agent in the conversion of energy from one form into another. As likely benefactor to an emerging celestial consciousness, the purpose of human society is to boost energy-conversion efficiencies to ever-higher levels,' M added.

'Where does a heightened sense of identity come from?' Phil asked.

'From the role a leader plays!'

'A leader?'

'No matter what the level, each of us is a leader in his or her environment.'

'Which roles do you have in mind?'

'Roles that help an organization move forward.'

'Forward?'

'Indeed, from one stage of behavior-pattern emergence to the next!'

'I'd sure be interested to know what my role is!' Eve said.

'Well, let's find out! It requires you to identify what your comfort zone is,' M said smiling.

'Why?' Phil asked.

'Because, your comfort zone determines what you'll do when push comes to shove.'

'I see!'

'I will summarize the four stages of behavior-pattern emergence but, now, with the role of the leader in mind. To broadly identify what your leadership comfort zone might be, you'll only need to decide in which one of these stages you'd be most at ease and most effective!' M said.

'All right!' Eve said on behalf of the group.

'I'll start with the second stage of behavior-pattern emergence, in which a triggering event induces the beginnings of orderly behavior after an inequality arises in the environment.'

The group appeared to make a mental note of this.

'When it comes to the emergence of a human organization, a triggering event involves a leader or entrepreneur who, inspired by developments in the environment, identifies a new idea—for example, a business idea, a product, a technology, a process, a theory, a societal model, or, even, a way of life, that might serve as a platform for future growth. Driven from within by conviction, this leader often needs to make several attempts before the idea has rooted, each time mending and presenting it until it eventually attracts the funds or votes needed to push it over a threshold. as it were. For identification purposes, I generally refer to this stage of human organization as *finding a new platform for growth.*'

Some in the group showed signs of recognition.

'What do you mean by a platform for future growth?' Phil asked.

'An entrepreneurial idea lies at the heart of all organizations which, in the process of becoming, generate growth; not just growth in revenue but also growth in services when it concerns nonprofit organizations.'

'Interestingly, an idea in itself is also a reflection of organization—that is, a cascade of neuron-cluster behavior patterns,' Chandra offered.

'You are quite right!

'In the next and third stage of behavior-pattern emergence, behavior patterns arise and the least-energy fitting survive.'

Phil and some others nodded in agreement.

'Typically driven by the needs of the market from without, a leader in this stage builds a straightforward organization, then galvanizes it by vision and passion, often not shy of airing the goal of wanting to change the world. To nurture nascent market niches, the leader cozies up to clients. Once an entrepreneurial idea has been transformed into a viable product or service, behavior patterns that appear to generate growth start out-reproducing others that don't. I refer to this stage of human organization as *resonating with the environment.*'

The reactions in the group indicated that they were starting to see the logic of the stages of human organization.

'In the fourth stage of behavior-pattern emergence, the role of a leader changes again. When a market niche develops into a viable source of demand, the challenge is to repeat success evermore efficiently. So to maximize the performance of an organization in this stage, a leader fans out part of his responsibilities to specialists, then weaves their activities into a seamless flow through processes and procedures. To ensure a steady stream of incremental improvements, he relentlessly nudges up the standards of success. Concerns for quality, cost, and capacity are at the center of frequent management reviews. No matter whether it concerns business units, processes, activities, or employees, leaders in this stage pick out the winners and let go the losers. To sway attitudes that are beyond their reach, they foster corporate culture. Eventually, a well-oiled machine of proven behavior patterns emerges that is capable of producing measured preprogrammed responses to signals received from inside and outside the organization. I refer to this stage of human organization as *repeating success evermore efficiently.*'

'What do you mean by corporate culture?' Phil asked.

'The collection of unwritten rules and norms that everyone appears to maintain and refer to. Something that would make employees say to outsiders: "Well, that's the way we do business here!"'

'Of course, I see!'

'In your description of the fourth stage, you consistently refer to a male leader. Is this stage indeed the domain of males?' Eve asked.

'No, not at all! You are quite right. Just assume that whenever I refer to "he" and "his" I also mean "she" or "her."'

Eve smiled disarmingly.

'Are you all still with me?' M asked.

An affirmative murmur arose from the group.

'We have now arrived at the first stage of emergence.'

'Why is that?' Phil asked.

'Because it naturally follows the fourth stage and explains how the second stage may arise again.'

'I see what you mean but I don't fully understand it.'

'You will soon, once I have explained why the first stage emerges.'

Phil nodded.

'At the end of the fourth stage, the dependence on preprogrammed responses, however much optimized, eventually erodes the ability of an organization to deal with unforeseen developments in the market, such as macroeconomic events and the introduction of new technologies, particularly when these developments minimize or even annihilate the very market inequalities that have sustained the business so far. The reliance on preprogrammed responses also fosters complacency as the dogma of corporate rules is likely to turn the collective perspective inward. When, as a result, growth starts to decline, these organizations are more than often incapable of shaking off their self-imposed straightjacket.'

'This is when a new type of leader should be appointed!' Eve noted.

'That's right! The role of a leader in this stage of behavior-pattern emergence is to break the back of prejudice and habit by confronting established ways of thinking and acting. This means unlocking an organization by simplifying and purifying it and by forcing it to search for standards of success outside. However, even when succeeding in making the business profitable again, this leader will not reinvent the organization nor will he return the organization to a growth path. At best, a level playing field is created from which new ideas may rise under another leader whose task it is to identify a new platform for growth in the next stage of emergence. In the world of business, however, a company in this stage doesn't often get that chance. The share price in this stage often fails to rise because growth falters. As a result, shareholders are tempted to force a leader to sell off the business. In short, I refer to this stage of human organization as *creating a level playing field.*'

'Rather than the first stage of emergence, this, to me, is more like the end of a business!' Phil noted.

'This can be both the end and the beginning of an organization.'

'How is that so?'

'The level playing field that is created is likely to contribute to the emergence of new organizations elsewhere.'

'Hmm, I see.'

'In summary, I have translated the stages of behavior-pattern emergence into the related leadership situations—that is, *finding a new platform for growth, resonating with the environment, repeating success evermore efficiently,* and *creating a level playing field.* Let's now see in which of these situations you feel most at ease and at your best. So who relates most to the second stage, *finding a new platform for growth?*'

An awkward silence followed. Then, a resonating murmur erupted when various people started consulting their neighbors. Some in the group stood out in that they quietly watched the interaction and refrained from participating. When the interaction quieted down a bit, Abdul raised his hand.

'I am most comfortable in this stage which might explain why I set myself the goal of seeking a new platform of thinking for the world in which I grew up. I believe that my example, *Ibn Rushd* or *Averroes,* if you'd like, would also have opted for this stage.'

'Thanks, Abdul! From what I gathered, I would also have identified you as a *transformer.*'

'A transformer?' Phil asked.

'That's right, a transformer! Leaders, who consider this stage as their comfort zone, are transformers because they are instrumental to the identification and acknowledgement of a fundamentally new idea that may function as a platform for future growth to their environment. In other words, such leaders help transform the premise of advancement in their environment.'

'This stage also represents *my* comfort zone,' Umberto said. 'As an academic, I have tirelessly worked on the definition of a new premise for future manufacturing technologies. My interest in the kind of discussions that we have had over these last few weeks confirms that I am still fascinated by fundamentally new insights that may facilitate the advancement of our world.'

One or two others also raised their hand and explained why they considered this stage to be their comfort zone.

'Thank you! This was most enlightening,' M said.

'To deepen our understanding of transformer-type leaders, can you give us one or two examples of public figures?' Eve asked.

'Sure!

'A transformer-type leader that comes to mind first is Prince Siddhartha Gautama, who is also known as "Buddha," the enlightened one. A compassionate leader of thought rather than religion, Buddha did not confront society nor he did he build one. Instead, he chose to search for an insight that would help ordinary people distance themselves from their daily suffering. After years of near-suicidal self-denial, he managed to reach beyond the appearance of physical reality and identified a way to its behavioral causes and conditions. In doing so, he became the first known thinker ever to unveil the behavioral nature of our world.'

'Do you mean to say that Buddha was an escapee?'

'Indeed he was! He did not allow anyone to return him to the cave and was one of the first to flourish outside the cave.'

The example of Buddha triggered a wave of reactions in the group.

'Abraham Lincoln, the sixteenth President of the United States, is another example of a successful transformer-type leader. In the United States, Lincoln is regarded as the president who newly founded the nation. The abolishment of slavery was the idea that energized him. Typically for transformer-type leaders, his life and political career were marred by failed attempts. When his election as president dawned on the nation, South Carolina and six other states, not agreeing with his condemnation of slavery, announced that they would leave the Union and form the Confederate States of America. In 1861, the Confederate States started a civil war when they attacked the Union. In April 1865, only Lincoln's fifth General-in-Chief, Ulysses S. Grant, succeeded in ending the American Civil War and restoring the Union. When Lincoln confesses that he didn't control the events but that the events controlled him, he shows himself to have been keenly aware that the course of his life depended on the emerging inequalities in the environment of his time.'

'It is maybe not surprising but still remarkable to hear that historical leaders knew that inequalities triggered the realities in their world,' Eve said.

'Let's go to the next stage of organizational development, *resonating with the environment*. Who feels most at ease or is at his or her best in this stage?'

Knowing the process by now, the group was noticeably more relaxed. Gabi was the first one to raise his hand.

'I probably feel most at ease in this stage. As I said, I am looking for a a new insight or a new philosophy. I am not the one that identifies such a new insight but the one that uses it to accommodate the need for a universal logic of existence that is felt across the sciences.'

Charlene was the next person to raise her hand.

'I believe I am a *builder* too. As human-resource director of my company and as academic, my focus is not on reinventing the wheel but on building the human infrastructure needed to advance my society in a sustainable way. To be really successful at that, I need to be at one with my target group.'

'Builder?' asked Phil.

'Leaders that identify most with this stage I simply call *builders*! The term expresses the essence of what these leaders do. Not unlike the other three types of leaders, a builder organizes matters in a way that he or she feels comfortable with,' M responded.

'It occurred to me that these stage-inspired comfort zones are rather fundamental because they are derived from the four universal stages of behavior-patterns emergence,' Eve observed.

'That is why I often call them *leadership archetypes* rather than just leadership types.'

'I think, I might also be a builder,' Zander said. 'I haven't had much time to prove it but, intuitively, I feel this to be the stage where I'll be at my best,' Then his face turned into a smile. 'In particular, the goal of wanting to change the world appeals to me!'

Rather than comment or smile, M looked Zander in the eye which seemed to indicate that, for one reason or another, he took his remark very seriously.

After the other builders in the group had introduced themselves, Eve asked M for one or two examples of public figures that were builders.

'According to the British historian, Paul Johnson, Peter turned out to be "a very unsteady rock on which to found a church." After the death of Jesus, Peter did not manifest himself as a leader and was pushed out of the Jerusalem circle by James, the youngest brother of Jesus. In 49 CE, during an assembly in Jerusalem chaired by James, only the passionate intervention by Paul prevented the sect from folding back into Judaism. Johnson describes Paul "as a beneficiary of a vision," a true builder who developed the ideas of Jesus about the interpretation of Judaic law into a theological framework that responded to the needs of both Jews and Gentiles throughout the Roman Empire.'[10]

'In my view, this concerns the *Son of God* and his *Word*, not an organization!' Abigail reacted, rather upset.

'In Jewish scriptures from the second century BCE, reference is made to "the coming of the *Son of Man* at the end of days." In his letters, Paul, who never met Jesus, yet knew about these scriptures, developed the *Son of Man* into the *Son of God*. Just as the scribes of many a King

---

[10] *A History of Christianity*, Simon & Schuster, 1976

introduced the *Gods* to reinforce their code of law, Paul introduced the *Son of God* to reinforce his teachings,' Chandra noted.

'Of course, the issue here is not belief. No matter who is behind the *Word*, it affects the behavior patterns of people who are guided by it. As such, the four stages of behavior-pattern emergence also describe the emergence of religion,' M said calmly.

Abigail didn't react. M looked at her to establish empathy but she ignored him.

'It is not surprising that the world of business produces exceptional builder-type leaders, considering its focus on growth. An outstanding example is Steven Jobs, the founder of Apple Computers. Starting from his parents' garage, Jobs managed to grow a 600-million-dollar business, surrounding himself with a highly motivated team of talented people. After having been ousted by a man he hired, Jobs eventually returned to Apple to kick start another cycle of growth. With an exceptional sense of what consumers wanted and a clear-cut vision of what worked and what didn't, Jobs identified market niche upon market niche, from the iPod and iTunes to the first "tablet computer" ever. As a builder-type leader, Jobs typically relied on a close-knit team and was involved in most product decisions. Considering the first-day sales of Apple's novel products, Jobs displayed an extraordinary ability to resonate with the market.'

A murmur of acknowledgement arose from the group.

'This brings us to the fourth stage of behavior pattern emergence, *repeating success evermore efficiently*,' Eve noted.

'Indeed! Who feels most at ease or is at his or her best in this stage?'

'Well, I guess, I feel most comfortable in this stage,' Eve said. 'To me the societal perspective is important. I worry about process. What can be done to involve people throughout all layers of society? How should you "package" ideas so that they encourage their own broad application?

'I second that! I also believe this to be my stage. In my country, it is crucial to reach out to people without provoking their cultural differences and premises of belief. So I am interested in ways that allow people to rise *above* their differences, ways that help them create a perspective not just of the collective but also of self,' Chandra said.

M turned to Abigail and looked at her without speaking. Briefly, she turned down her eyes and thought to herself, 'What does he know?' Then, she decided to share her hunch.

'As a theologian and Christian, sacred scriptures are at the center of my interest and life. How does the divine reach out to us through these scriptures? What does he expect from us beyond his commandments? On consideration, I feel most at ease in this stage because it is about following established rules and preprogrammed responses that should prevent us from leaving the divine path to heaven.'

'Forgive me for asking, but won't this clinging to rules and responses eventually prevent societal phenomena from advancing to the next stage of their emergence?' Phil asked.

'I can't tell. I am confused, to say the least, by insights that seem to undermine the timelessness of religion,' Abigail responded.

'Why?'

'It is in conflict with what I solidly believed throughout my life.'

'So your belief is in the way?'

'To me, my belief still *is* the way!'

'Then, what will you do with the knowledge of the *path of Emzine*?'

Abigail smiled shyly and shrugged her shoulders, 'I don't know yet.'

Phil barely managed to hide her feelings of despair.

'Before you ask me again, Eve, let me give you two examples of public figures that are *growers*. By the way, I refer to leaders that show this type of leadership as *growers* because they tend to create the conditions for stable growth through specialization and optimization.'

'Of course!' Eve said, grateful to M for bringing the dialogue back on course.

'Muhammad proved to be a *builder* who developed the Jewish and Christian scriptures into a collection of memorized verses that fit the needs of the Arab world. Like other builder-type leaders, "he personally controlled every detail of organization, judged every case, and was accessible to every suppliant." In less than a decade, he realized his vision of bringing the Arabian Peninsula under Allah's rule. According to the Sunnies, Abû Bakr or *Abdullah Ibn Abi Qahafa*, an old friend of Muhammad, was elected as rightful leader. During his reign, which lasted a little more than two years, Abû Bakr invaded both the Sassanid Persian Empire and Eastern Roman or Byzantine Empire. As such, he paved the way for one of the largest empires in history a few decades later. Abû Bakr not only expanded the territory under Islamic control but also established the administrative infrastructure needed to repeat early success more efficiently. He instigated preprogrammed responses by publishing an authorized Koran and by founding a body of Islamic law involving specialists, from his generals to financial controllers, as part of an all-inclusive process. By all standards, Abû Bakr emerged from history as a true grower-type leader.'

Abdul looked at M straight-faced, not showing any sense of pride. This did not go unnoticed and must have added to his stature in the group as an independent leader of thought in his field.

'My second example comes from the world of business again.'

'Why, may I ask?' Phil asked.

'Shareholders get excited by rising share prices and only growth will make share prices rise. So in the world of business, leaders who manage a stage of rising or stable growth tend to be remembered.'

'I see!'

'One of the most-lauded and innate growers in the world of business was Jack Welch, CEO of General Electric during the last twenty years of the second millennium. During his reign, Welch grew the company's market value more than twentyfold. The papers started referring to him as *Neutron Jack* when he fired more than 100,000 employees. He also sold or closed down numerous businesses, maintaining and buying only those ranking first or second in the market. Welch particularly focused on the improvement of people and processes, committing the company to the largest total-quality program ever in Corporate America. Nudging up the standards of success ruthlessly, he told his team to identify the company's top and worst performers. While the latter executives were fired, the former were trained by him personally. Fascinated by military discipline, he hired hundreds of young army officers annually. On the whole, Welch created and sustained an exceptionally process-driven organization that excelled in repeating success evermore efficiently.'

'No doubt, the intent of Welch was to create an organization that would last forever,' Phil noted.

'That's what he probably believed or hoped for! He did not expect his "growth machine" to falter. Much to his surprise, I am sure, it did a few years after he left the company. Of course, no leader can build an organization that lasts! The question is how can one help leaders benefit from this controversial piece of knowledge,' Charlene said.

'Our discussion will converge on that question soon. For the moment, though, we have the first stage of behavior-pattern emergence left. Who feels most at ease or is at his or her best when *creating a level playing field*? Who is the *confronter* or *purifier* among us?'

Without a word being said, everyone in the group spontaneously turned in the direction of Phil, who initially did not notice that she was the target. The moment this dawned on her, she smiled and put her hands up as if they were all pointing guns at her.

'I admit, I behaved as a confronter during our meetings. I am indeed focused on shaking the tree of jargon to let the true meaning of what has been said fall through. You know, many of you bring a wealth of preprogrammed responses from established environments that are truly meaningless to me. So this was, in part, self-defense. I did not have a university education. Due to circumstances, my life and interests veered in more mundane directions. Then again, I will tell you this, by bringing you down to level Earth, I have learned *so* much! Now that I think about it, by constantly asking for clarification, I may indeed have contributed to the conditions for the creation of a level playing field, an environment or state from which a new platform of societal growth may rise.'

Again, Phil managed to stun the group by the articulated and subtle way in which she formulated and analyzed her own comfort zone. Both Umberto and Eve realized how much Phil had learned *and* contributed.

'I'd be quite interested to know the public figures that have the same comfort zone as I,' Phil added laughing.

'Mind you, the obsession for growth in the world of business explains why innate confronter-type leaders are often ignored. Who wants to admit to corporate decline? As a result, grower-type leaders, handpicked by their predecessors to keep their companies on a growth path, are forced to assume a confronter-type leader role when they are served the sour grapes of decline,' Charlene noted.

'Dwight Eisenhower seems to have been an exception. As General of the US Army in World War II, Eisenhower excelled in confronting the leadership of the enemy and undid what they had done. As presidential candidate, Eisenhower promised to continue his confronter-type leadership by undoing the policies of President Truman. He vowed to end the Korean war and establish an administration that would be corruption free and prudent in its spending. As president, Eisenhower kept his promises and did more. "He saw to the cease-fire of the Korean War, kept up the pressure on the Soviet Union during the Cold War, made nuclear weapons a higher defense priority, launched the Space Race, enlarged the Social Security program, and began the Interstate Highway System." On the whole, Eisenhower succeeded in creating a level playing field from which a new societal wave could rise under the transformer-type leadership of John F. Kennedy.'

Phil seemed satisfied with M's example.

'On the other hand, Jeffrey Immelt was handpicked by Jack Welch as his successor. Not long after his appointment in 2001 as CEO of General Electric, Immelt was forced to assume a confronter-type leadership role when the company's growth rate declined. Selling under-performing businesses, as Welch once did, was not always an option. Some of GE's divisions had grown so much that no company could afford them at the time. Immelt chose to confront and purify the company, trying to create a level playing field from which a new cycle of growth might emerge. This seemed to explain the renewed interest in the company's research capabilities. In 2005, Business Week reports that "the changes are tough for the many who aren't dreamer types," a trait that seemed unthinkable during the reign of Welch who rather hired military officers. In 2007, Immelt managed to sell GE Plastics, the company's largest division that groomed both Immelt and Welch! In 2009, General Electric lost its triple-A rating as well as US$ 264 billion in market value. The international press then realized that GE, under Welch, "did not groom super managers after all." Immelt secured the company's profitability, in this stage of behavior-pattern emergence. But, he may yet fail to restore growth. At best, he may hand the company over to a successor who will transform the business. Alternatively, the rumor of "a more valuable GE when divvied up" may persuade shareholders to carve up the business. At some point, the growth of its share price was indeed less than that of the S&P 500 and far below that of Siemens.'

'When I listen to these striking examples, many things go through my mind. This process for analyzing organizational change and leadership does indeed provide insight, especially the overlay of growth patterns with leadership archetypes,' Eve observed.

'I even used it to identify my role within my family, my university, my company, and my community. I imagine that this would also be a very helpful schema for family counselors!' Charlene added.

'I am particularly intrigued by the promise of prediction that comes with the steady stages of organizational emergence,' Chandra said.

'You mean the ability to anticipate the problems and solutions in an imminent stage of development?' Eve asked.

'Indeed! If you'd know the signals that hint at the coming of the next stage of corporate and, even, national emergence, you would probably ease the process of societal evolution!'

'...and, make the transition more efficient at the same time!' Eve said.

'That's right! The question is what are these signals!' Chandra said.

'Considering the examples discussed so far, *growth rate* clearly is an indicator of the next stage emerging. It is the canary in the coal mine!' Charlene said.

'The canary in the coal mine?' Phil asked.

'Miners used to bring canaries into coal mines because they would be the first to faint when the amount of methane gas rose to fatal levels. In other words, canaries would warn the miners when to take the necessary precautions.'

'Oh, I see! So what would be the rate of growth in organizations that traverse the first stage of behavior-pattern emergence?'

'Well, an organization that *is in search of a new platform of growth* traverses a stage of *uncertain growth*—that is, either uncertain revenue growth or uncertain services growth in case of a nonprofit organization.'

'The hand of a *transformer-type* leader must be behind this, right?'

'Yes, and no! The rate of growth is more a reflection of the stage of organizational emergence than of the leader. On the other hand, during each stage, leaders necessarily play a certain role.

'So, what does a *transformer* do?'

'The one thing that leaders *can* do!'

'And that is?'

'Point the awareness in their organization in a direction that is key to the natural selection of the most appropriate behavior patterns.'

'I'd think that leaders do much more than that! Don't they make bold decisions, for example?'

'They do but, in practice, not until they know that the organization is ready to acknowledge and execute these decisions. This requires them to persuade their organization that such a bold decision would benefit its development.'

'In which direction do transformers point their organization?'

'They help an organization search its inner *self*. Which capabilities, competencies, and ideas does it have and how might these serve as a new platform for growth? In other words, transformers effectively turn the focus of their organization inward!'

'How do they pull that off?'

'Transformers rely on *belief* to motivate their people. Necessarily driven by intuition rather than fact in this stage, transformers cannot say much more than, "Yes, we can!" Transformers use belief as the *social force* that gets and keeps their people going, as it were,' Charlene said.

'So, conversely, if an organization is *inward looking, ruled by belief* and experiencing *uncertain growth* then it must be in the first stage of behavior-pattern emergence,' Eve said.

'At the same time, you'd know that the next stage of emergence involves *resonating with the environment* and *rising growth!*' Charlene added.

'And, a *builder-type* leader, no doubt!' Eve noted.

Charlene nodded.

'So, what do *builders* do to ensure that their organization resonates with the environment?' Phil asked.

'Builders orient their organization to the market environment. What does the market really need? Which developments are suppliers working on and how can these be used to minimize market inequalities? In other words, builders turn the focus of the organization outward!'

'How do they motivate employees?'

'Builders typically rely on *vision*. What will this organization have achieved when people do their job well?' So they use vision as the social force that gets and keeps people going.'

'Hence, if an organization is *outward looking, ruled by vision* and experiencing *steadily rising growth* then it must be in the second stage of behavior-pattern development!' Eve noted.

'Right! Again, you'd also know that the next stage of emergence will involve *repeating success evermore efficiently; stable growth;* and a *grower-type* leader,' Charlene added.

'Here I go again! How do *growers* ensure that success is repeated evermore efficiently?' Phil asked.

'Growers help their organization to analyze the inner *self* again and to identify ways in which it might improve its functioning. They raise the question of which people and processes it ideally needs. So like transformers growers turn the focus of their organization inward, albeit for a different purpose!'

'How do they motivate their people?'

'They use the combined force of *culture* and *rulebooks*. Driven by fact rather than intuition in this stage, growers pursue the compilation of rules of success that people should adhere to. To ensure the follow-up of less-tangible rules, they also foster a culture. So culture and rulebooks are the social forces that get and keep people going in this case.'

'Hence, if an organization is *inward looking, ruled by culture and rulebooks*, and experiencing *stable growth* then it must be in the third stage of behavior-pattern emergence!' Eve noted again.

'Indeed! At the same time, you'd know that the next stage of emergence will involve *creating a level playing field, declining growth,* and a *confronter-type* leader. You'd be back where you began in the cycle of emergence!' Charlene said.

'I should know, being a confronter, but how do *confronters* ensure that a level playing field is created?' Phil asked.

'Confronter-type leaders reorient their organization to the external environment. What are the standards of success out there and how can they be used to simplify the organization and level it with competitors? Like builders, confronters turn the focus of the organization outward, but now it is to restore profitability!'

'How do *they* motivate employees?'

'Confronter-type leaders introduce *open-mindedness*. Which market standards should the organization embrace to become profitable again?' In other words, they use open-mindedness as the social force that gets and keeps people going when turning the business around.'

'It is striking to see how the polarity of leadership direction is changing from one stage to another,' Chandra noted.

'You mean, the outward and inward orientation of an organization in subsequent stages of organizations?' Charlene asked.

'That's right! It's Nature breathing inward and outward again!' Chandra said, remembering the Mount-Nelson exchange where she first used the breathing metaphor.

'This yin-yang effect is indeed essential to the process of behavior-pattern emergence and thus to the emergence of what we call reality,' M said.

'It also occurred to me how much each stage of emergence is focused on the establishment of the most opportune patterns of behavior,' Chandra added.

'This might explain why leaders do not outgrow organizations but why organizations outgrow leaders!' Charlene suggested.

'Why is this so?' Phil asked.

'Leaders remain stuck in their comfort zone while organizations advance from one stage to the next,' Charlene explained.

'That sure is a sea change in the common interpretation of the role of leaders—I mean, leaders being effective for a limited amount of time only until their organization or nation advances to the next stage of its emergence!' Eve noted.

'When the canary faints, they should make room for a successor with a different type of leadership!' Chandra concluded.

'Of course, this effectively also means that the outgoing leader is not the best person to select the next leader!' Charlene said.

'Why is that?' Phil asked.

'Well, considering the ego of many a successful leader, leaders tend to seek successors in their image and this is exactly what might keep their organization from advancing!'

'Why, again?'

'If you'd bring in a leader with the same comfort zone as the previous one while the organization is steadily advancing to the next stage of its emergence then this leader will instill behavior patterns that belong to the stage that the organization is departing from!'

'So, leaders rather than organizations are at the end of the tail when Nature wags its tail?'

'That's a way of describing it.'

'So, beware! You shouldn't judge an organization by its leader but a leader by the state of his organization or nation!' Eve added.

'Hmm, yes again!' Charlene said.

'Then, what is the role of a leader?' Phil asked.

'Considering the *path of Emzine*, the role of a leader is to help bring an organization from where it is to where it should be on its path of behavior-pattern emergence. Effectively, leaders do not create or cause anything, rather they help create the conditions and awareness needed for an organization to self-create, as it were,' Charlene responded.

'Relating to our world is so much more meaningful now that I know the comfort zone of each of you and what to look out for when it comes to organizations!' Umberto observed.

'I agree. You know who you are!' Phil added.

'You also know how you relate to your organization!' Umberto noted.

'What's more, you know how you relate to your peers!' Eve added.

'And, so do your peers!' Phil said with a wink.

'What I find most intriguing is that you know how future success can be achieved!' Umberto said.

'From a human-interaction point of view, you also know when and when not to dominate a discussion,' Charlene said.

'Why is that so?' Phil asked.

'Well, you should not dominate a discussion when the organization is traversing a stage that does not line up with your comfort zone. Your assessment of problems and solutions would simply be out of tune.'

'Of course, I see!'

'The possibility of identifying what makes "role models" successful is perhaps one of the most pertinent benefits! I'd also be keen to learn which strategic relationships work,' Umberto said.

'What do you mean by that!' Phil said.

'Well, I'd be interested to know the stage of emergence of each of the companies or countries that appear to be collaborating successfully!'

'Oh, I see!'

'This is particularly also useful to *diplomats*, I figure! They might use this knowledge to fine-tune their foreign policies,' Eve reacted.

'Here is what I'd do. I'd color code the stages of emergence and the comfort zone of leaders,' Umberto said.

'What value does that add?' Phil asked.

'Well, I imagine that if you showed on a map the stage of emergence of nations and the comfort zone of their leaders by means of a color code, it would be easier to distinguish the match between leader and nation. Of course, you can do the same for companies and their leaders!'

'I gather that if you also depicted in this map successful strategic treaties, you'd learn which color combinations work best,' Eve added.

'This reminds me of the iconoclastic psychologist, Clare Graves,' Charlene said. 'A contemporary of Maslow, Graves identified various levels of human development, each level involving certain behavioral traits and human values. As in Maslow's hierarchy, the higher the level the more advanced you are. Yet, contrary to Maslow, Graves believed that societies might move up and down his hierarchy depending on the conditions. Interestingly, the work of Graves made a breakthrough only after his death when Don Beck—one of his more street-smart followers— had shrewdly linked each level of human development to a specific color. This considerably increased the visual appeal of Graves's hierarchy and fostered its use as behavioral map and human-value strategy tool. When Beck eventually reported about the use of this color code in the design of post-Apartheid South Africa, Graves's hierarchy finally became recognized as a society-development tool.'

'That confirms my hunch!' Umberto said. 'Collective development-stage evaluations might even be made part of the repository of knowledge on the Internet. Tomorrow's search engines might use these to generate color-coded maps with the development stage of nations, regions, companies, and religions and the comfort zone their leaders!'

'No doubt, this would make human society more conscious of how it might help Nature develop our world!' M concluded. 'Then again, the danger is that the meaning behind these color codes might eventually be forgotten. Remember, the same happened to our perception of time! Hours, minutes, and seconds began standing on their own when man lost the realization that time emerges from a relation between two events—an event of which you'd like to measure the duration and a reference event that is recurrent. This is why I'd suggest to be prudent when using color codes. We should never forget what is behind them!'

At this point M realized how long the discussions had gone on.

'We have talked at length about the effects of simultaneity outside the cave but I have lost track of the time gone by in the back of the cave! We haven't even touched our picnic baskets! So allow me to wrap up today's most interesting exchange!'

The group reacted harmoniously.

'We discussed in practical terms what the effect of the *path of Emzine* is, particularly its effect on organizations and their leaders. During our discussions, it occurred to me that, when it comes to organizations, the benefits of the behavioral explanation of existence comes in three simple measures: *Unification*, *Predictability*, and *Reinforcement.*

M looked around to gauge the group's response.

'*Unification* means all phenomena of organization can now be related because, whatever the actors involved, they concern behavior patterns.

In other words, by reducing all phenomena of existence to emerging behavior patterns, you can now compare apples to apples!'

A murmur of acknowledgement arose from the group.

'*Predictability* means that, once you identify the actual stage of behavior-pattern emergence, you know which stage will unfold next including its problems, solutions, and leadership needs.'

Again, the group produced a loud murmur of assent.

'*Reinforcement* means that independently emerging phenomena of existence can now be made to reinforce one another through temporal alignment.'

'Temporal alignment?' Phil asked shyly.

'Temporal alignment means aligning two or more phenomena of existence that happen to traverse the same stage of behavior-pattern emergence. An example of reinforcement is coevolution.'

'Coevolution?'

'The term "coevolution" emerged in biology to describe situations where the change of one species triggers the change of another species. Thus, coevolution means that the emergence of one behavior-pattern species triggers the emergence of another behavior-pattern species.'

'Do you mean to say that one form of existence *causes* the emergence of another form? As I recall, systems theorists refer to this as "mutual causality!"' Eve said.

'That is indeed the term used but it's wrong!'

'Why?' Eve asked surprised.

'Nothing really *causes* the emergence of anything else! Emerging behavior patterns create the conditions for the emergence of each other! Remember, outside the cave, *simultaneity* rather than an unmoved mover is at work! Simultaneously emerging behavior patterns inevitably function as conditions for the emergence of each other. However, this is *reciprocal conditioning* rather than mutual causality!' M said.

'Buddha summarized this eloquently. "*[Matters] arise together and only together they arise,*" Chandra said.

A silence fell on the group as each person considered this idea.

'We have made tremendous strides today particularly regarding the emergence of organizations. So what should be on our agenda next?'

'We should now focus on the effect of the *path of Emzine* on the individual,' Charlene suggested.

'This would be consistent with the four stages of emergence, which indeed depend on the conduct of individual actors, particularly at the beginning and end of a cycle of emergence. Your suggestion tells me that we are nearing the end of our dialogue!'

'Why particularly focus on individuals?' Phil asked.

'When behavior patterns cascade to repeat success more successfully, the environment sustained by this waterfall of patterns "railroads" the conduct of human actors involved. When this cascade eventually breaks up due to a changing environment, these actors are on their own. Then, the question is what should determine their conduct. This is what Charlene is essentially referring to, I think.'

Charlene nodded in agreement.

The group looked confused initially, then the quarter dropped.

'One more question?' Phil asked.

'Sure!'

'What type of leader are you?'

M smiled openly.

'Let me give you a hint! Only after several attempts did I find the *path of Emzine*. It will no doubt take several attempts again before *the path* is acknowledged broadly.'

'I guessed it right, I think!' Phil said.

'You sure did!'

From Meta-Awareness To Meta-Morality

Eager to evaluate how the *path of Emzine* might affect individuals, the group had agreed to gather soon. The suggestion was to meet at the Morgenster or Morning Star estate, one of the neighboring olive farms. Together with Lourensford, Morgenster was once part of the Vergelegen or Faraway farm, which the Dutch Cape Governor, Adriaan van der Stel, an employee of the Dutch East India Company, had established some three hundred years earlier. When, in 1708, van der Stel was called back to the Netherlands by his employer after complaints from local farmers about unfair competition, the property was divided into four farms. The Frenchman, Jacques Malan, a Huguenot who had fled persecution by the Catholic Church, bought one of these estates and gave it the name Morgenster. At the time of the gathering, the owner was an Italian business man. Craig Cormack, the chef of the estate's cottage restaurant, was kind enough to host the meeting.

When everyone had arrived, Phil welcomed the group with a brief explanation of the estate's history.

'Jacques Malan named the Morgenster estate after Venus, one of the brightest objects in the sky in the morning. Considering Malan's history as refugee, the Morgenster label must have been highly uplifting to him. You see, according to the ancient Greeks, Venus was "Phosphoros" or the "bringer of light,"' Eve offered.

'What's more, the ancient Greeks identified Venus as two separate bodies, as Morning Star *and* Evening Star, the latter being "Eosphoros" or the "bringer of dawn,"' Chandra added.

'Of course, by now, we know that *Phosphoros is Eosphoros*. These are two different aspects of the same planet!' Umberto observed.

'Two different aspects?' Phil asked.

'Well, one aspect might be a name that you'd use to refer to an object and another might be a term that you'd use to identify the sense of an object,' Umberto responded.

'This is all very philosophical!'

'Well, if I were to mention the name "Hoover," you'd know which object I am referring to, right?'

Phil nodded.

'If I were then to mention the term "vacuum cleaner," you'd also recognize the object,' Umberto continued. 'Of course, this might not be a Hoover and this is what language philosophers typically worry about.'

'I see what you mean, kind of,' Phil said, not wanting to belabor the topic.

'Couldn't you say that the true meaning of *human being* arises from the terms or aspects, *good* and *evil?*' Abigail asked, not really expecting an answer.

Everyone looked at Abigail, surprised by what initially appeared to be a change of subject.

Abigail innocently put up her hands, 'The thought merely occurred to me when I realized that the Latin word for Phosphoros is "Lucifer," the name of the fallen archangel!'

'To be faithful to history, the Bible does not refer to Lucifer as evil or devil. Reference is made to an over-powerful King of Babylon who stands in the way of the Israelites. The prophet, Isaiah, simply promises that this King is like the Morning Star and, thus, destined "to fall from the sky," as it were! The transformation of Lucifer into the devil evolved after the Biblical texts saw the light and has in part been attributed to works of fiction,' Chandra was quick to remind the group.

'Our world hasn't changed much in some respects!' Abigail said, apparently referring to the historical situation of the Israelites.

So far, M had quietly watched the discussion unfold.

'It seems, our meeting place inspired the beginning of our dialogue again! What does the discussion remind you of, thus far?'

Eve was the first to react, her mind rushing back to the first time she'd met M.

'Now that I think about it, we behaved like prisoners that are chained to the walls in the back of a cave. I am so embarrassed at getting carried away by theories of our own making about the meaning of paths in the sky. It feels like trying to read the faint features of echo and light on the walls in the back of the cave again.'

'Not to worry, it got us to the question of human conduct, which is what we have on our agenda today!'

Eve smiled with relief.

'Wait a minute! Malan was an escapee, wasn't he? So what made him read the sky again, as it were?' Phil interjected.

'Although Malan managed to escape from the cave of Catholicism, he sought refuge in another cave, the cave of Protestantism.'

'Why did he?'

'He did not know about the moral ground that might have supported him outside the cave!'

'Moral ground? What ground are you referring to?' Phil asked.

'The term "morality" stems from Latin and refers to proper behavior. Moral ground is the logical premise that we use to decide whether our intensions and actions are either good or bad.'

'So, unaware of the moral ground outside the cave, Malan could do nothing but enter another cave!' Phil concluded energetically.

'That's right!'

'What would have supported him outside the cave?'

'Well, what do you think?'

'All I know is that, outside the cave, the emergence of inequality in the environment triggers the emergence of behavior patterns.'

'Isn't that enough?'

'I don't get you!'

'I mean, the external conditions determine our behavior *and* what we think is good or bad! That should be enough, I figure!'

'I am not sure whether I follow you, let alone agree! The Ten Commandments apply in all conditions, in my view,' Abigail interjected.

'Do they?'

'Yes, I believe they do!' Abigail responded resolutely.

'So, in the sixteenth and seventeenth century, it was immoral of the leaders and followers of both the Catholic Church and Protestants to persecute people whose opinion about faith differed!' M said.

'The situation was different at the time!' Abigail protested.

'So, you are telling me that the conditions *did* play a role and justified the persecutors to break the commandments.'

'It was wrong to break the commandments but it had to be done!'

'Why?'

'Because it was God's will!'

'Both Catholics and Protestants subscribe to essentially the same Ten Commandments. How can God be upset by that?' Eve asked, surprised.

'The root of the problem was *in the way*!'

'Aha, *the way*! Which way?'

'God's way!'

'Well, at the time, the root of the problem initially was in the way of the Catholic Church!' M intervened.

'I don't understand,' Abigail responded.

'As we discussed at Lourensford, the Church or any movement, for that matter, is a form of organization that develops according to the four stages of behavior-pattern emergence. Particularly, when organizations reach the fourth stage of emergence, problems tend to arise!'

'Why is that?'

'In the fourth stage, organizations are tempted to replace the need *to become* by the need *to be*!'

'I don't follow you!'

'In the fourth stage, organizations, such as the Catholic Church at the time, are focused on reproducing success more efficiently, typically by the development of preprogrammed responses to signals from inside and outside. Yet, the dependence on such responses eventually also erodes the ability of organizations to deal with new societal inequalities.'

'Why?' Phil asked.

'In the end, the justification for the existence of an organization is less found in emerging societal needs and more in the perpetuation of established organizational rules and practices. Once the dogma of rules and practices turns the organizational perspective inward, complacency develops. Then, the question no longer is what can be done to advance the organization in view of the inequalities in the environment but what can be done to sustain it.'

'So, the sweet smell of success appears to be addictive!'

'That's a way of saying it!'

'So, what happened?'

'Christianity had become a business that was centered on the trade of fake relics, indulgences, special privileges, masses for the dead, and assertions of salvation, all in exchange for money. The Catholic Church thrived on a theology that was based on dogmatic statements derived from mistaken readings of ancient texts that had not been examined for centuries. The secretary of Pope Nicholas V went as far as referring to the Church's key texts as "blatant forgeries."'

'The Protestant movement must have been very welcome,' Phil said.

'In what sense do you mean that?' Eve asked.

'Well, it must have responded to the needs of the people!'

'Initially, it did! The Protestant movement translated ancient biblical manuscripts into local languages and, in this way, freed the ordinary man from the self-centered interpretations by the Church,' M said.

'Why initially only?' Eve asked.

'Once the Protestant teaching became established as a state religion, it too became intrusive. People, who did not believe, were driven to the sermon. In 1531, Luther even stated that "those who do not fit in should be done to death by the civil authority." The Protestant movement gave people access to early texts, which it then blindly drove down the throat of willing and unwilling followers, not prepared or able to evaluate their true value, in spite of evidence of heavy tampering in even the earliest manuscripts.'

The group digested this piece of history in silence.

'Don't all religions experience eras in which religious scriptures are followed to the letter however out of perspective or out of date?' Abdul asked after a while.

'As forms of organization, religions inevitably will!'

'This really shakes the ground under morality, I'd say,' Umberto said.

'It might not when you give it a closer look!'

'In that case, what moral ground might support escapees outside the cave?' Umberto asked.

'First, morality involves behavior patterns that are perceived as either good or bad. Hence, outside the cave, morality is bound to contribute to the observable reality on the path of Emzine.'

'So?' Phil said.

'Outside the cave, the premise of reality is that inequalities in the environment trigger the emergence of behavior patterns. The driving force behind reality and, therefore, morality is the minimization of inequalities by least-energy fitting behavior patterns. Incidentally, as we discussed at OYO, physicists captured this force in the abstract laws of thermodynamics.'

'Of course!'

'Putting my assertion the other way around, during the four stages of behavior-pattern emergence, emerging behavior patterns, whatever the visible features of existence that they produce, ought to minimize inequalities in the environment as fast as the local conditions allow. It is immoral if they don't!'

'That is my understanding, indeed!'

'Well, human organizations and their leaders have a habit of seeking refuge in the very cave of behavior patterns that they help establish during a particular stage of behavior-pattern emergence. In traditional evolutionary theory, this is referred to as niche construction.'[11]

'So, what?'

'Well, when leaders help organizations select the least-energy fitting behavior patterns during a certain stage of emergence, these behavior patterns will eventually narrow the collective perspective to such an extent that they will prevent these organizations from advancing to the

---

[11] John Odling-Smee, *Niche Construction*, Princeton University Press, 2003

next stage of emergence when different behavior patterns are needed. Understandably, in a way, the leaders in these organizations are often not inclined to change behavior patterns that have been shown to lead to success in the past. They may even be tempted to hire consultants or the "civil authority" to reinforce these behavior patterns when they seem to slacken but, as these leaders are bound to discover eventually, to no avail. As you can imagine, at that point, established behavior patterns function as a behavioral niche or cave, from which it is hard to escape.'

'Why is this so bad?'

'As the Catholic Church and the Protestant movement showed, when forms of organization and their leaders become so inward looking that inner needs prevail over the emerging needs in the environment, this will be to the detriment of the environment, as a whole, and of the followers in particular.'

'Why are you picking at religions all the time?' Abigail asked.

'You are right! I should not give you or anyone, for that matter, the idea that I am. Indeed, the same applies to all forms of organizations, from religions, nations and political parties to companies and charities.'

'What typical examples are you thinking of today?' Phil asked.

'Totalitarian regimes are particularly prone to this. As still too often is the case, in nations that are not allowed to continue on their natural path of emergence, the suffering can be horrendous because societal inequalities are not minimized effectively.'

'So, the morals of leaders are at stake here!' Abigail noted.

'Leaders are typically seen as exponents of organizational strategies and, in some respects, they are. However, forms of organization are not really about leaders but about cascades of behavior patterns. Leaders or, for that matter, totalitarian regimes depend on cascades of established behavior patterns and are powerless without these. This is why these unfortunate situations cannot be improved overnight.'

'So, you are telling us, "it's the organization, stupid!"' Phil concluded.

'What, in sum, does the moral ground outside the cave involve?' Umberto asked.

'It boils down to one primal rule, that is, to ensure the continued emergence of least-energy fitting behavior patterns that will minimize inequalities in the environment as fast as the local circumstances allow.'

'Then, how do you achieve this?

'By preventing forms of organization, including the behavior patterns of neural networks behind our thoughts, from getting stuck in stage-inspired behavior-pattern caves.'

'I see your point but how?' Umberto asked again.

'By creating awareness, not just awareness of the necessary behavior patterns in a particular stage of emergence but also awareness of how behavior patterns will need to change from one stage to another. The awareness of behavior-pattern development across the four stages of emergence is a form of meta-awareness, meta meaning across.'

'Remind me again, when do behavior patterns need to change?'

'When the canary in the mine no longer sings!' Charlene offered, referring to the dialogue at Lourensford about signals, such as the rate of growth, that indicate when the next stage of emergence looms.'

'Aha, of course!'

'So, morality relies on meta-awareness or a keen eye for the entire path of behavior-pattern development. Meta-awareness helps prevent the development of stage-addiction, an addiction that undermines the emergence of least-energy fitting behavior patterns; the effective minimization of inequalities; and the opportune development of our world as a whole.'

'The opportune development of our world, as a whole, is a matter of both morality and economics. In business, least-energy fitting behavior patterns are the nature of a firm because they essentially reduce the transaction costs when minimizing inequalities in the market.[12] What's more, the effective minimization of inequalities will improve what the philosophers, Jeremy Bentham and John Stuart Mill, identified as "the measure of individual satisfaction or utility!" Bentham and Mill argued that utility is "a moral criterion" for the organization of society. So, feeding on the ideas of Bentham and Mill, the effective minimization of inequalities in the environment involves matters such as economic

---

[12] Inspired by Ronald Coase, *The Nature of the Firm*, Economica, November 1937

freedom, the separation of church and state, the freedom of expression, the abolition of slavery and the death penalty, and the equal rights of women,' Charlene added.

M waited to let this sink in, then made a surprise statement.

'Meta-awareness covers only half of the moral ground outside the cave!'

Apart from Charlene, everyone looked slightly puzzled.

'Why?' Phil asked.

'The nature of behavior patterns in each stage is different, and so is the notion of good and bad behavior,' M added.

'Are you, by any chance, referring to our discussion at Lourensford again?' Eve asked.

'I am! To deal with stage-specific challenges, some of the least-energy fitting behavior patterns in society will necessarily change from stage to stage. In other words, behavior patterns that are perceived as desired in one stage may be felt as inappropriate in another.'

'Will you please refresh my mind again?' Phil asked.

'As you'll recall, I mentioned that, in successive stages of emergence, the orientation of an organization will alternate not unlike yin and yang between an inward and outward focus. Similarly, the orientation will alternate between the need for fundamental and incremental changes, the need for integration and fragmentation, and, as so vividly illustrated by the boom-bust cycle of the world economy, the need for borrowing and saving.'

'The distinct types of leadership across the stages of behavior-pattern emergence also indicate that the perception of good and bad behavior is bound to change each stage!' Charlene added.

'Then, what covers the other half of the moral ground outside the cave?' Umberto asked.

'Considering that the perception of what is right and wrong depends on the stage of behavior-pattern emergence, the other half of the moral ground outside the cave must involve meta-morality, meaning the understanding that our notion of what is moral and what is not will and must change across the different stages of development.'

M looked around the group to gauge their reaction.

'As an escapee, how do you go about dealing with meta-awareness and meta-morality?' Phil asked, finally.

'Escapees need to balance meta-awareness and meta-morality—that is, meta-morality to facilitate the development of stage-specific ideas of right and wrong and meta-awareness to prevent getting stuck in stage-specific behavior-pattern caves.'

'Considering what you just said, it occurred to me that escapees should ideally try to transform behavior-pattern caves into behavior-pattern cocoons!' Chandra noted.

'Why?' Phil asked.

'A behavior-pattern cocoon gives shelter to behavior patterns that are sustained during a certain stage of emergence eventually to give birth to a behavior-pattern cocoon for the next stage. So, during each stage of emergence, some behavior patterns are spun that will function as rudimentary cocoon for the next stage later on.'

'The behavioral cocoon metaphor is truly imaginative, indeed! As I will illustrate later, science might well have produced evidence that supports your hunch,' M said appreciatively.

'To me, this doesn't in any way correspond to the Ten Commandments!' Abigail observed.

'This is due to the longstanding dichotomy between the perspective inside and outside the cave. Probably handed to Moses by the divine in a figurative sense, the Commandments are inside-the-cave abstractions of what is believed to be the divine premise of good behavior outside the cave. So the question is whether and in how far the Commandments agree with the premise of good behavior that escapees subscribe to outside the cave,' M said.

Abigail nodded hesitantly, not really trusting the inside- and outside-the-cave distinction.

'The Ten Commandments can be divided in two broad types of rules. Depending on the Abrahamic religion in question, the first two to three rules dictate the relationship with God while the last six to seven rules prescribe the relationship with man, particularly one's parents, spouse, and neighbors. The third or fourth rule dictates a day of rest for worship and reflection. In view of its rank, this rule effectively links the higher and lower-ranked clusters of rules... Are you still with me, Abigail?'

'Yes, I am,' Abigail responded, barely audible.

'Let's examine the first two to three rules. Inside the cave, the notion of God is reality, no doubt. Labels, such as God, Allah, Yahweh and so on, would not have emerged if that had not been the case. After all, what really is the notion of God? What I am trying to say is that we should identify the emperor, not his clothes nor the other ways in which his grandeur is transmitted.'

M noticed signs of anxiety in the group.

'Considering what we know about the world outside the cave, the force exerted by the opaque complex of inequalities, that determines the course of the world outside the cave, must have induced the notion of God in the back of the cave. This explains why God appears to rule the world in ways that puzzle the cave prisoners. Of course, this force is evidence of Nature's search for least-energy fitting or "good" behavior patterns on the path of Emzine. So God is Nature and Nature is God!'

Nobody reacted; many held their breath.

'Nonetheless, outside the cave, the new, participative and increasingly articulated relationship with Nature is bound to replace established theories about the divine that were inspired by the faint features of echo and light on the walls in the back of the cave.'

"Why?' Phil asked.

'Essentially because they are superfluous!'

'So, to become an escapee, I will need to leave my faith behind!' Abigail mumbled, yet loud enough to be heard.

M turned to Abigail.

'You don't need to deny your religious past to become an escapee. After all, it brought you to where you are now! Then again, you don't need to become an escapee. It's entirely your choice!'

For a moment, Abigail looked beaten, realizing that further denial would be beyond her reach at this point.

'We will explore what determines your choice later on,' M offered.

'So, what about the Commandments that deal with the relationship with man?' Phil asked, trying to steer the dialogue back on course.

'The path of Emzine replaces the other Commandments in that it generates the understanding needed to respect behavior patterns that are induced and sustained by cascades of inequalities in the world outside the cave. Of course, the path of Emzine does not specify exactly what escapees should or should not do but it educates them about the exact nature and importance of behavior-patterns relations, including those involving humans.'

This reminds me of Matthew (13:1-23) who stated that "with understanding comes accountability!"' Zander offered.

'Outside the cave, God is no longer there to help us make a distinction between good and evil. It's all up to the escapee! How will this prevent people from sinning?' Abigail asked, trying a new line of inquiry.

'Thus far, God has not prevented large scale sinning throughout our world. Maybe an improved understanding of the emerging nature of the world outside the cave and a better sense of our role in the process will! After all, least-energy fitting behavior patterns largely represent "good" behavior,' Chandra observed.

'Why do people sin or err?' Phil interjected.

'Why do behavior patterns develop anyway?' M asked in return.

'In response to certain environmental conditions!'

'That's right! Our actions are defined by evolving conditions over lengths of time, I mean, inequalities in the environment as well as those inside our body and brain. Behavior patterns, that are triggered and sustained by these inequalities or conditions, may cascade at many levels, in multiple ways, and far beyond our awareness and control to produce what we would qualify as either good or bad behavior.'

'This turns my perspective of morality upside down! This means it isn't fair to punish people that display bad behavior because you know that their behavior is an inevitable consequence of physical and societal conditions,' Eve said.

'Considering that punishment deals with the symptoms rather than the cause, it seems even immoral!' Charlene added.

'I share your observation! Punishment essentially means blaming the messenger for certain conditions!' M said.

'At some point, you might want to contain rather than punish bad behavior to prevent it from contaminating society. I know, this is easier said than done. When should you contain someone? Of course, I am not worried about locking up a serial killer but, when political opponents are involved, containment becomes tricky!' Umberto said.

'I guess, meta-awareness helps you identify those situations where leaders try to preserve stage-specific behavior-pattern caves by locking up opponents!' Charlene noted.

'When it comes to serial killers and the like, bad behavior should ideally be prevented and corrected by creating the right conditions. I imagine that this might involve tweaking both physical conditions, even at the level of faulty DNA, and societal conditions,' Chandra offered.

'In my view, one should try to create conditions that prevent the emergence of bad leaders as much as one should try to create conditions that prevent the emergence of serial killers!' Eve added.

'Outside the cave, you'd probably be in a better position to do so but even then Nature will not let you be completely successful,' M said.

The group looked puzzled. Phil was the first to react.

'If the force of Nature is about the selection of least-energy fitting or good behavior patterns then why does it allow bad behavior patterns to emerge?'

'Because that is in the interest of Nature!'

'In the interest of Nature?'

'I'll give you an example later on but here is a quick answer. During the selection of least-energy fitting behavior patterns, some patterns that take more energy to fit are also produced as possible parent contributors to future behavior-pattern cascades. In other words, Nature keeps some higher energy fitting or "bad" options in the loop because their offspring might contribute to least-energy fitting cascades in the future.'

'So, to a certain extent, less than optimally fitting behavior patterns or "errors" can be functional!' Eve said.

'That's right! Errors in the broadest sense of the word may function as gateways to new behavior-pattern cascades and, even, worlds by what they are or cause directly or indirectly. So, rather than evil or sin, there is error outside the cave!'

M paused briefly, then offered what appeared to be an afterthought.

'Remember the cocoon metaphor? At the heart of the rudimentary cocoon that is spun for the next stage, you may find behavior patterns that are considered as "erring" in the current stage.

'I believe this whole idea is flawed!' Abigail said, apparently convinced that she'd found a loophole.

'In what way do you mean this, Abigail?' M asked.

'If our behavior is indeed the inevitable consequence of physical and societal conditions then we are not in control of our own actions. You don't want to tell me that I do not have "free will," do you?

'You are not the first to realize this! The philosopher and Nobel laureate of literature in 1937, Henri Bergson, noted that "in cases where action is freely performed, we cannot reason about it without knowing the conditions that caused it. If our actions are pronounced by us as free, it is because we do not understand the relation of this action to the state from which it is issued." According to Bergson, our notion of free will is indeed an illusion.' [13]

'That was in the first half of the twentieth century!'

'Recently, the neuroscientist, Sam Harris, an authority on what might be called the *science of morality*, came to the same conclusion. He argued that "our belief in free will arises from our moment-to-moment ignorance of specific prior causes. All of our behavior can be traced to biological events about which we have no conscious knowledge: this always suggested that free will is an illusion." Harris refers to research, which illustrated that "conscious decisions can be predicted up to *10* seconds before they enter awareness." So, although we appear to be aware of our options, "we are not the authors of our actions."' [14]

'If we don't have free will, then who or what are we?' Phil asked, somewhat concerned.

---

[13] *Time and Free Will*, Dover, London, 2001

[14] *The Moral Landscape*, Free Press, New York, 2010

'As we discussed at Mount Nelson, man is one of Nature's most complex exponents in the minimization of inequalities. So, turning the matter around, we should consider ourselves fortunate that our role comes with a sense of awareness. Of course, Nature allows us to witness its process of becoming consciously to provoke our contribution. Then again, in return for the growing realization that we are but reflections of conditions, we can improve our grasp of past, present, and future.'

'In that case, what choice do I have?' Abigail asked desperately.

'What *is* choice?' M asked in return.

Abigail shrugged her shoulders.

'Considering that our actions and decisions hinge on previous and current conditions, *choice is the momentary awareness of one's path of becoming. It's a glimpse of your destiny.*'

'One's path of becoming?' Phil asked.

'It's the path of the directions that you take either consciously or subconsciously.'

'Directions inspired by previous and current conditions?'

'That's right!'

'So, I do not have a choice but a destiny!' Abigail pronounced with an alien twinkle in her eye.

M caught what she'd said and responded, 'Previous and current conditions will determine the choices you'll make in the future. They'll decide your destiny.'

A door opened and Craig Cormack stepped out onto the verandah of the restaurant. He headed straight for where M was seated and whispered something in his ear.

Alchemist No More

Craig smiled broadly when addressing the group, 'Our restaurant is not officially open today but, since I am around anyway, allow me to make you a light meal based on what I find in the fridge so you can continue your most interesting dialogue.'

'Thank you, Craig!' Phil said enthusiastically and turned to the group.

'Craig is a true kitchen alchemist. He knows how to transmute even the most basic of ingredients into gold for tongue and taste!'

'Craig reminds me of Newton, one of the greatest scientists that history produced,' Gabi noted when Craig had left.

'Why?' Phil asked, slightly puzzled

'In his book, *Principia*, Isaac Newton describes the law of universal gravitation and the three laws of motion, which functioned as the groundwork for classical mechanics. For three centuries, Newton's laws were at the core of explanations of our physical world.'

'What does that have to do with Craig?'

'Well, however unlikely it may sound, Newton, a key contributor to the emergence of hard science, eventually became absorbed by occult studies. The substantial amount of mercury found in his body after his death not only explains that mercury poisoning must have produced his eccentric life style when he grew older but, also, that, as an alchemist, Newton must have tried to make gold by mixing base metals.'

The group appeared to have no clue of where Gabi was heading.

'So, the common view of our world today essentially is an *alchemist's perspective* which assumes that our physical world consists of parts that somehow move, mix and react together.'

'Not to forget, a physical world that consists of parts or things that, we believe, can also be made to move, mix and react together!' M added.

'Of course, the view of the world at the core of our dialogue is truly different!' Gabi concluded.

'You mean, we are living in a wholly behavioral world where physical appearance and things are byproducts of consistently repeating behavior patterns in the fourth stage of behavior-pattern emergence?' Phil said, checking her version of this worldview again.

'That's right! By the way, Malan developed this estate just about when Newton worked on the second edition of his *Principia*. In this edition, Newton uses his famous phrase, *hypotheses non fingo* or *I contrive no hypotheses*, to state that motion alone rather than an occult agency causes gravity. Isn't it coincidental that we meet at this very estate to finish our dialogue about a new worldview!'

Most in the group seemed to share Gabi's amazement.

'What people often don't realize is that Newton was highly religious. He wrote more on the interpretation of the Bible and occult studies than on the scientific groundwork that he is remembered for. He was not an escapee, so to speak,' Chandra added.

'Apparently, the physical and nonphysical worlds were believed to be two different things at the time of Newton. This sure is in contrast to the worldview outside the cave. Outside the cave, there is no distinction between the physical and nonphysical. The emergence of behavior patterns explains both, whatever the actors, remember?' Eve noted.

'The question that I'd like to raise is about the difference of approach in the back of the cave and outside the cave. If prisoners in the back of the cave follow an approach that reminds us of alchemists then what is the approach of escapees reminding us of?' Chandra asked.

'Let's assess first whether and how far the alchemist still lives on in today's world,' M said.

'Material science, which focuses on the discovery of materials with special properties, initially depended on an approach that reminds me of alchemists,' Gabi said.

'What exactly does this approach entail?' Eve asked.

'Tinkering! Tinkering with materials, mixing methods, temperatures and other environmental conditions hoping to identify new materials. Many a new material emerged by chance this way. Researchers would typically backtrack the process, guessing what might have happened, to reproduce their accidental findings.'

'As I understand it, the haphazard search for new materials is gradually being replaced by a more fundamental approach,' Umberto said.

'That's right! Increasingly, material scientists are looking into the thermodynamics behind the structure of atoms. This gives them more control over the achievement of certain material properties that depend on structure.'

'As I recall, at OYO, you explained that thermodynamics involves the behavior of actors when energy is converted from one form into another, right?' Phil checked with M.

'Indeed! Thermodynamics involves motion and, thus, behavior.'

'So, when it comes to material science, the behavioral side of material existence is gradually getting more attention. Out of necessity, material scientists are leaving the cave!' Gabi said.

'Strangely enough, when it comes to obvious behavioral phenomena, such as organizations, we are still tinkering. Too often, leaders and their advisors appear to be chained to walls in the back of the cave!' Charlene noted.

'Do you mean to say that there is a need for a thermodynamic or energy-based assessment of behavior patterns in organizations?' Phil asked.

'Like material scientists, leaders and their behavioral scientists will get more control over the properties of an organization once they start investigating the thermodynamics behind people structures.'

'You mean, structures consisting of least-energy fitting behavior patterns?'

'Indeed! The focus on procedures that help improve the performance of an organization indicates that the need is there.'

'Regarding our discussion at the Foodbarn in Noordhoek, I guess the charter of the *science of emergence* would include such investigation,' Eve noted.

'I would think so! Gabi guided our discussion to a field that also explains why it is in the interest of Nature to produce a certain level of bad behavior. Remember?' M said.

The group signaled acknowledgement.

'The Russian scientist, Artem Oganov, probably the most prominent expert in crystallography today, developed a fairly straightforward, yet exceptionally effective algorithm that can be used to predict the least-energy fitting atom structure for a selection of different atoms based on their individual properties.'[15]

'What is an algorithm?' Phil asked.

'An algorithm is a set of instructions that tells a computer how to calculate something.'

'Hmm, I see!'

'While identifying lower energy fitting combinations of atoms, Oganov's algorithm keeps on producing higher energy fitting or bad combinations until the least-energy fitting structure has been found, that is, a structure involving all the different atoms or actors.'

'Why is that?' Eve asked.

'The higher energy combinations add to the landscape of potential combinations that the algorithm will wander through when searching for ever-lower energy combinations of combinations. So higher energy fitting or "bad" combinations are functional in that they broaden the landscape of potential atom combinations and, this way, speed up the search and selection process.'

'A mouthful but I see your point!' Eve said with a smile.

'Anyway, the appearance of least-energy fitting selection in Oganov's algorithm shows that the behavioral nature of atoms has firmly entered the equation for material existence.'

'How true an observation, Eve!'

---

[15] *Modern Methods of Crystal Structure Prediction*, Wiley-VCH, 2010

'Isn't that what happens when, in a particular stage of emergence, a behavioral cocoon is spun for the next stage?' Chandra asked.

'In what sense do you mean this?'

'Well, a cocoon for the next stage involves behavior patterns that may be "bad" in the stage in which they emerge, yet are functional in that they add to the landscape of potential future patterns!'

'That's right!'

'I am confused, to say the least,' Phil said. 'If behavior patterns survive that are not least-energy fitting then Nature doesn't follow the least-energy fitting principle!'

'I understand your confusion,' M said, 'but, as I mentioned at Mount Nelson, less optimal behavior patterns may survive in "neighboring" niches with slightly different conditions where they continue to influence the process of natural selection on the *path of Emzine.*'

'So, what does the approach of escapees remind you of?' Chandra asked.

'What do *you* think?'

'Escapees are alchemists no more. They mix and mould no longer blindly. They experiment with behavior patterns rather than things.'

'When historical rulers expound the behavioral requirements in their back-of-the-cave empire by whose authority do they do this generally?'

'By the authority of what they'd call "the creator!"'

'Escapees are creators! The reality observed on the walls in the back of the cave will, in part, be a reflection of what *they* cause!'

The Philosophers' Dream

In the departure hall of Cape Town Airport, M stood in the check-in queue for the next flight to Europe. Eve was waiting outside the check-in area. M preferred traveling light. When it was his turn, he soon received his boarding ticket, not having to check in any luggage. He then looked around searching for Eve who had walked to two empty seats near the entrance to the departure gates.

'These have been a remarkable few weeks!' Eve said when M was seated next to her.

'You can say that again! Not just remarkable but also instructive! I feel so relieved!'

'Why is that?'

'These ideas have been roaming inside my head for years.'

'I guess they must!'

'I am particularly grateful that I've had the privilege to scrutinize, grow and transmit these ideas all at the same time through the collective efforts of a group that emerged almost magically each time we met!'

'I've got one question left!' Eve said.

'You are kidding me, Eve!'

'No, I am not! Remember the first time we met?'

'How could I forget!'

'Well, you mentioned that the behavioral worldview would provide oxygen to the ideas of important philosophers. You said it as if you'd personally met these philosophers.'

M smiled, realizing that the dialogue had made a lasting impression, 'Sure, I remember! I "met" these philosophers *again* the night following our final session at Morgenster.'

'Is that so?' Eve said, wondering for a fraction of a second whether M was pulling her leg.'

'I have apparently nosed into the work of these philosophers so much that my mind made them appear alive and well in my dreams. I must say, each time, I woke up with a retro-perspective of my own ideas as an unexpected bonus.'

'Tell me!'

'I met the same philosophers as the first time around but now in a different setting.'

'In South Africa?'

'No, in Tuscany, Italy.'

Eve looked fascinated.

'We met on the verandah of Il Borghetto, a beautiful ancient Tuscan villa in the rolling vineyards close to San Gimignano, right at the center of where the mysterious Etruscan civilization emerged in pre-Roman times some 2700 years ago. Il Borghetto's owners and wonderful hosts, Riccardo Bimbi, his sister, Sandra, and their respective spouses, were all waiting at the villa's entrance gate to greet me. Riccardo, who looks a bit like a philosopher himself, led me to the verandah. The villa is the ultimate stage for a meeting with a distinct group of deceased sages.'

'What was it like—I mean, meeting these philosophers?'

'When I arrived, I saw three men in light grey cloaks busily chatting. Considering what they were wearing, they were evidently ancient Greeks. Two other, more contemporarily dressed men were sitting at the same table. Their exchange was more subdued. They were the first to notice me when I arrived.'

'Then, what happened?'

'When I took a chair and sat down with them, the Greeks looked up, slightly irritated, no doubt because of my interruption. The eldest Greek spoke to me first.'

"What can we do for you?"

'I assumed that they knew why we met. So I asked him whether they had had a chance to listen in.'

"Listen in?"

"Our dialogue!"

"Of course, we did! What is it that you'd like to know?"

'If this is their attitude, I thought, I'd better set the rules.'

"Sir, I am sure that there are many things that you might not relate to or that you'd question but we simply don't have time for that now. So what I'd like to suggest is that you briefly explore what in the dialogue seemed to reinforce your own findings."

'The old man looked at his Greek compatriots and then at the two other men. All nodded in agreement.'

"Sir, if you don't mind, will you please introduce yourself first?"

"I am Anaximander, once a citizen of the town of Miletus in what is now Turkey. As I recall, 2600 years ago, the traders were already talking about the wares of the Etruscan people in this region."

'Anaximander paused briefly, searching for a start.'

"I am not sure whether my honorable friend, Theophrastus, who is sitting next to my neighbor, Parmenides, has been interpreting my work correctly. From our brief chat just now, I gathered that he is bound by the things he observes, in my view, too much!"

'Theophrastus smiled politely.'

"As I unfortunately learned, only a meager 6 lines of my prose have survived to today. What makes it worse is that they have been tinkered with to an extent that they have become opaque! Had I known this then, I would probably not have put so much effort into writing! Then again, I probably would have because it was in my nature to do so."

'The others laughed.'

"I have travelled many a time in what you'd call an Eastern direction. On my travels, I met wise men who inspired me. Their views on the

endlessness of existence, however short our experience of human life, brought me to identify the Boundless. The Boundless is an impersonal thing. It's both immortal and unborn. See it as an ever-flowing fountain, a primal state of chaos from which everything springs. At the same time, it is an inevitable abyss where everything perishes. I found no reasons for qualifying the Boundless as either space or time."

"In what way did the dialogue resonate with the Boundless, if it did?"

"Well, I recognized the Boundless in the endless cycles of four stages of behavior-pattern emergence, patterns that generate both space and all that it may contain. The dialogue made me realize that the Boundless is essentially a behavioral phenomenon. What we experience and observe, including the space in which we live and the time that we measure, are reflections of reproducing behavior patterns. What truly fascinated me is the elegant distinction, and the connection between what we observe inside the cave and what causes it outside."

"Thank you, Anaximander! Of course, we should be grateful to Plato for transmitting Socrates's Allegory of the Cave."

"Sure but the dialogue truly broadened and deepened its meaning!"

'Theophrastus' face radiated pride and understandably so because Plato had once been his teacher.'

"Parmenides, may I invite you to share your comments?"

"As you said, I am Parmenides. Like the Etruscans, I was an inhabitant of what is now called the Italian Peninsula. Some 2500 years ago, I lived in the South, in the coastal city, Elea, which was then part of Greece."

'Parmenides smiled wearily.'

"I share your frustration, Anaximander! Only 5 percent of my poem, On Nature, made it through history and then, of course, the degree of misinterpretation! Not really being a poet, I wrote poetry to lower the threshold towards my teachings. I introduced mythical characters to relate to the realm of interest of my audience. Yet, my efforts to adjust to the context of my world have been ridiculed by blunt and biased eyes that appear to have been seduced by the visible features of our world."

'Parmenides composed himself.'

"I disagreed with my contemporaries about the essence of our world. Heraclitus, for example, became fascinated by change. Indeed, you don't step in the same river twice. The moment you step in again, the river has changed. However, that is inadequate and even nearsighted. While focusing on how a river changes all the time, you lose perspective of the fact that all rivers are reaching for the sea. That is where the true nature of our world lurks.

"Our observations are subjective. We observe our world in a way that is not unlike the eyes that viewed my work through a veil of alien experiences. The All that I call Nature is objective, impersonal and, in our eyes, even ruthless. It has nothing to do with what we experience as being. When I talk about Nature being timeless, uniform, necessary and unchanging, I don't think of our observations and experiences. These traits are not meant to be transposed into our experiential world."

"So, how did the dialogue resonate with your view of Nature?"

"When I visited Athens at a rather old age, I met a young man with whom I had a similar discussion."

"Aha, you mean Socrates!"

"That's right, Theophrastus, that was his name! Well, I hope I didn't waste my time."

"You didn't Parmenides! It is through Socrates and his pupil, Plato, that your ideas reached us. Your views sparked successive explanations of our world and might even have inspired the Allegory of the Cave."

"I am starting to feel a bit better now! Back to your question, how did the dialogue resonate with my ideas? The metaphor of the cave clearly resonated with my explanation of Nature as a duality—that is, Nature as we subjectively experience it in the back of the cave and Nature as it is outside the cave. According to Theophrastus, I may have contributed to this notion. So that probably explains why it resonated."

'Everyone laughed.'

"The dialogue confirmed my notion of Nature being timeless. Time is a human invention. If anything, simultaneity rather than time is relevant to Nature. That brings me to being. Nature simply is! It is in a constant state of simultaneity. To Nature, the motion that we observe and even cause is not motion but some progression from simultaneity to simultaneity. To *calculate the motion of an object from A to B, you need to have some measure of time but Nature doesn't have a clue! Driven by inequalities, it just progresses. This progression involves constant becoming from one stage of simultaneous behavior patterns to another. So, to Nature, to be means to become."*

'Parmenides's articulated comments surprised the other sages.'

"At some point, I reasoned that thought and being are the same. Well, the dialogue confirmed that the behavioral nature of our world outside the cave explains both the physical and nonphysical. Indeed, the progression of simultaneous behavior patterns is at the heart of thought as much as it is at the heart of a flower."

"What about Nature being uniform, necessary and unchanging?"

"If Nature were changing, it would have an idea of what it needs to change to! In other words, it would have some sense of temporality and purpose. As the dialogue confirmed, Nature hasn't. For lack of a better word, each instant, it has a sense of necessity based on the state of inequalities. So you might say that Nature involves necessity. However, don't read too much into this. Think about the two connected containers where molecules spontaneously start moving in a direction where they are least obstructed. If anything, to Nature, the movement of molecules is progression, a sequence of simultaneity states.

Finally, I suggested that Nature is uniform. Considering the diversity of Nature, I can imagine why people are confused, to say the least, when they read such a bare statement but, remember, nearly three thousand lines of my poem, On Nature, have vanished. As the dialogue reiterated, the uniformity of Nature is not in the diversity that it produces in the back of the cave but in its way outside the cave. The uniformity of Nature is in the path of Emzine!"

"Thank you for your exceptional analysis, Parmenides!"

"Theophrastus, may I invite you to contribute your comments?"

"Certainly, you may!"

"Forgive me for asking but why did you volunteer to attend this meeting rather than your teacher or your teacher's teacher?"

"You mean Plato or his teacher, Socrates?"

"That's right!"

"I will let you know my reasons but let me introduce myself briefly first. I was born some 2400 years ago on Lesbos, a Greek Island near the coast of Turkey. At an early age, I moved to Athens to become a pupil of Plato. It is there that I became a friend of Aristotle, one of Plato's other students. When Aristotle died many years later, he left me his library and made me the guardian of his children. I headed his school for thirty-six years as his successor. I had the good fortune to reach a ripe old age. Nonetheless, I felt that my life was much too short. When it comes to our insight, we die just when we are beginning to live."

'Theophrastus' observation made the other philosophers chuckle.'

"I admit, Aristotle and I focused on what we experience in the back of the cave. You can only guess what might be taking place outside the cave. At least, that is how I reasoned then. We wanted to unveil the logic behind the world that we observed. For example, we figured that a substance is divisible into other substances. If not substances, there must be attributes, and if attributes, attributes either of man or of some other subject. On the whole, my views appear to be in line with those of Aristotle. However, in answer to your question, I volunteered because my views differ in ways, however subtle, that seemed relevant to your dialogue. I may add that it was I who studied the doctrines of Greek philosophers before Plato sometimes based on no more text than what is available today. This is why I feel responsible for these analyses."

'Parmenides smiled his concurrence.'

"So, how does the dialogue seem to resonate with your views?"

"Aristotle and I believed that existence essentially involves motion. Considering that behavior patterns involve motion "whatever the actors involved," the dialogue evidently resonates with our views. However, I differed with Aristotle when it comes to time. I saw time as an accident of motion rather than as an independent principle next to motion. In that, I believe, the dialogue reinforces my views rather than those of Aristotle. Time is indeed a figment of the human mind. In view of reproducing behavior patterns that become visible in the fourth stage of emergence, I believe that simultaneity or simultaneous motion rather than time is fundamental to the explanation of existence."

'The two men in more contemporary clothes seemed to agree.'

"My views deviated perhaps most from Aristotle's when he tried to explain why motion occurred. Contrary to Aristotle's view, I could not find enough reasons to conclude that all things happen for the sake of an end. Aristotle wanted to trace back the phenomena of our world to some ultimate cause which led him to claim that a prime mover set everything in motion. This might well explain why his ideas rather than mine were embraced by late medieval thinkers in their hunger for an independent affirmation of the divine. However, as the dialogue confirmed, there is no need for a prime mover because, from instant to instant, Nature is propelled by the circumstances of the present.

"I hope this explains why, in the end, I decided to volunteer."

"It certainly did, Theophrastus! Thank you for your most informative insight."

'I turned to the other two gentlemen, both bald and unpretentious, one with a small moustache.'

"Whom may I invite?"

"I guess, it is my turn since I was born about two years before my distinguished colleague, Alfred North Whitehead, who is sitting next to me. My name is Henri Bergson. I was born in 1859 in the month before the publication of Charles Darwin's On the Origin of Species. In other words, I grew up and lived in an era in which we started thinking about existence as a process of development rather than as a divine creation. As you can hear, I am a Frenchman. I ended up teaching philosophy at the Académie des Sciences Morales et Politiques in Paris."

"No doubt my distinguished colleague, Bergson, is too modest to tell you that he has frequently addressed audiences across the world and was awarded the Nobel Prize for Literature in 1927."

'The man with the moustache smiled shyly.'

"In your dialogue, you have already referred to my views about free will. So I'll continue the argument where Theophrastus left it. I too believe that motion is at the heart of existence. When I thought about the effect of motion, I saw freedom and duration. Mind you, by duration, I do not mean the idea of time that people use in the back of the cave. Like Theophrastus, I

believe that duration is an accident of motion rather than a principle that stands on its own."

'Theophrastus clearly appreciated the consistency of argument.'

"As the dialogue illustrated, the more deeply we study the nature of motion, the better we understand that movement and, thus, duration means invention, creation of forms, and continuous elaboration of the absolute new. On the path of Emzine, duration involves the endless production of observable reality. In this process, each instant of reality stands on its own due to the evolving conditions. History contributes to the unfolding of reality but wrapped in the conditions of the present. Because reality emerges in the present from one instant to another, our world of being is really a world of becoming."

"Thank you Professor Bergson, particularly for emphasizing that Nature is a process that is driven entirely from the present! Where will you take us from here, Professor Whitehead?"

"I'd say in the direction of the place where the dialogue took you. However, let me introduce myself first. I was born and raised in the United Kingdom. I taught mathematics at Trinity College in Cambridge. Near the end of my career, I was fortunate to be offered a position at Harvard where I pursued my interests in philosophy. I have had the doubtful honor of having been one of the most-quoted but least-read philosophers of my time, probably because my views differed from those of the scientific establishment at the time.

"Regarding the observations of my distinguished colleague, Bergson, I'd like to reiterate that simultaneity rules the present as much as it rules the world outside the cave. This leads me to the two main premises behind my views about the nature of our world.

"First, whether it concerns events or, as you pointed out, behavior patterns, simultaneity is the ultimate factor of Nature—I mean, simultaneity of events and behavior patterns.

"Second, the spatial order that we observe emerges from some temporal order, which in itself must involve simultaneity because of my first premise.

"These two premises indeed resonate with the views of Nature explored in your dialogue. Whereas I speak of temporal order, you speak of four stages of behavior-pattern emergence that hinge on and produce simultaneity."

"How did your views differ from the more established ones?"

"Briefly, present-time science is ruled by what I called the "dogma of materialism." Abstractions of objects or things, such as points of space and time, are considered more genuine than the relations that cause them. As a result, the reality of a magnetic field is derived from such point-like measures rather than from the field of relations that produces it. To me, this is misplaced concreteness! Physical or, as you said, observable matters, such as electromagnetic phenomena, are relational wholes that may reach across the universe.

"Having rejected points of space and time as abstractions of reality, I argued for events as abstractions instead. This is not unlike what you argued for. You illustrated that the reality that we observe is but a byproduct of repeating behavior patterns. Your dialogue also debunked time as an abstraction of reality. Time is a human invention and does not stand on its own. To Nature, only simultaneity matters. Do not get me wrong; "points of time" will remain meaningful to us when predicting the trajectories of things that move on the walls in the back of the cave. Yet, as an abstraction, time confuses rather than adds to the explanation of reality outside the cave.

"I might add that space is a human invention too. On the path of Emzine, motion and memory appear as more fundamental abstractions of reality, memory being repetitive motion. Motion is what you'd see when Nature reacts to inequalities from one state to the next. Space or, rather, our sense of space occurs when and where motion occurs. We lost our perspective of this somehow and started considering our sense of space as something that stands on its own. Of course, losing our perspective of the fact that space emerges from motion is like losing our perspective of the fact that time emerges from the willful translation of one occurrence of motion into another occurrence of repetitive motion.

"Here is where our views meet. I argued that the process of Nature and, thus, reality involves events that are entangled in relational structures. In *view of this interconnected nature of reality, I concluded, just like you, that the process of becoming is essentially an organizational phenomenon. This is why I referred to my theory as a "philosophy of organism" and predicted that such a philosophy would help us re-imagine and reinterpret our world. This is exactly what has happened! The path of Emzine is a philosophy of organism, indeed."*

"Thank you Professor Whitehead. Your reflections and those of your distinguished colleagues are most inspiring!"

'Two men approached the verandah. Riccardo guided an older man with thick silver hair and a clean-cut silver beard. I soon realized who this man was, a man whose line of heritage may go back to the Peruzzi's, a pre-Medici family in nearby Florence. So I hastened to introduce him to the group of sages.'

"It is a great surprise to see you here, Umberto!"

"So it is for me, M! We have just arrived. Phil is unpacking but I couldn't wait to sit in and listen. Please, forgive me for my interruption."

"We have nearly finished our session, Professor!"

"That's a pity. I would have loved to learn about your reflections."

"May I ask, Professor, as you have participated in the dialogue from very early on, what is your concluding perspective?"

"Of course, Theophrastus!

"As a meta-science, the Emzine theory will, in my opinion, prove to be instrumental to the prediction of processes of emergence. Predictions will not only be guided by the succession of four stages of behavior-pattern emergence but, also, by a more calculated projection of contextual differences and similarities. We can now refine our understanding in the sense that we will be able to predict how certain conditions may interact and reinforce one another and how they will play out, as it were."

"Doesn't that bring back the alchemist in us, Professor?"

"At first sight, one would think so. However, I am convinced that this won't happen. After all, no matter whether it concerns socioeconomic, physical or, even, mental conditions, the path of Emzine ensures that conditions will always be translated into behavior patterns, either into patterns that produce these conditions or into patterns that follow these

conditions. There is no doubt in my mind, behavior patterns along with the least-energy fitting criterion will push us into the role of creator."

"I think you have convinced me, Professor. Not that you had to drag me over a threshold, of course!"

'Theophrastus signaled that he wanted to make a closing remark.'

"Considering what I have learned so far, I believe that the dialogue has advanced the topic to a stage where the idea of Emzine may arise as a new and unifying theory of our world, a theory that goes beyond present-day science and religion."

'This is when I woke up from my dream. I would have paid gold to hear the reaction to the closing statement of Theophrastus. I tell you, I almost started believing that what I experienced was true.'

'I can imagine! By the way, I didn't understand Whitehead's remark about space. What about an empty room? That's space, right?'

'If space were really empty, you wouldn't see it. It wouldn't be there! You can observe an empty room simply because it is not empty!'

'How's that?'

'Our sense of empty space emerges from the motion of photons or electromagnetic wave packages that sustain it. Indeed, the present-day perception of space creates more questions than it answers. If "space" were an abstraction of reality that stands on its own and does not depend on motion then what is "non-space?" Similarly, if the universe involves such "space" then what is the "outside" of the universe about?'

'Hmm, these questions are trump cards to theologians, no doubt.'

Both Eve and M had completely forgotten about the time, at least until the airport announcer called for the passengers on M's flight to board. After a hasty goodbye, M rushed to the entrance that led to the airport gates.

Just before he disappeared, Eve shouted, 'Where will you be flying to?'

M could only half hear what Eve was saying but read her lips. 'To Rome! Didn't you know?'

The Conference

Eve was having a cappuccino at Java in Stellenbosch, as she often did. She was glancing through The Economist, which had arrived by mail the day before. She realized that the cover story about the fall of regimes in North Africa was so much more meaningful to her now. The article was a perfect case study of what M had explained about the inevitable and predictable development of forms of organization, such as nations, and the role of leaders. These regimes destroyed their nation by clinging on to power for too long and, as a result, failed to let the least-energy fitting behavior patterns of good governance arise spontaneously in successive stages of emergence, a process that requires courage rather than greed. Removing such regimes and their leaders would only be a beginning. Without the cascades of behavior patterns needed for good governance in place, such a power vacuum might well serve as a niche for another rogue regime. This is where meta-morality comes into the equation.

She was absorbed by the matter so much that she failed to notice Zander who had approached her table.

'Hi, may I join you?'

'Sorry, I did not see you coming! Sure, have a seat!'

'Did you take M to the airport?'

'Yes, I did and, as usual, he surprised me with a revelation just before his departure, almost missing his flight to Europe in the process.'

'A revelation?'

'He told me he had a dream, a dream in which he met five prominent deceased philosophers. His account of that virtual meeting was not just remarkably articulated but also showed how much the *path of Emzine* resonated with the views of these men.'

Eve gave a detailed account of what she remembered.

'"A unifying theory that reaches beyond present-day science and religion!" How inspiring!

'What does "beyond present-day science and religion" mean, do you think?'

'Not competing with but adding to present-day science and religion, I guess. At the same time, not dividing but unifying!'

'So, where do we go from here?' Zander asked.

'I asked myself the same question but I don't know! What can you do? Whatever you do will just be a ripple in a river that needs to find its own way to the sea!'

'I guess, you are right! Too bad!'

'Then again, what makes anything happen in this world?'

'An inequality, I guess!'

'Hmm, how do you create an inequality that invites the spontaneous development of behavior patterns?'

'In my opinion, the inequality is there. The world is ready for the *path of Emzine* but it doesn't realize it yet.'

'So, someone should take the trouble to inform the world about it?'

'That's right!"

'How?'

'By writing a book on the story of Emzine, for example!'

'Hmm, that sounds like an interesting idea!'

'You were the first to meet M. Why don't *you* write one?'

'I am beginning to understand why M once said that I would be "the mother of a new understanding."'

'There, you go!'

'I'll think about it.'

'Such a book might also help spread the *idea of Emzine* and trigger new scientific research.'

'Tempting, indeed!'

'However, to foster a new awareness, it must be accessible too.'

'You mean, an awareness of how the various phenomena of existence relate.'

'That's right!'

Ten years later, the night before a major international conference was to start in Cape Town to commemorate the coming of a new era, M arrived on a flight from Europe. A chauffeur was waiting in the arrival hall and took him to the conference-center hotel. After checking in, M retired to his hotel room. Sitting in one of the room's armchairs, he studied his speech notes one more time and then went to bed, knowing he would have a busy day ahead of him. Normally, his thoughts would roam from topic to topic before his mind would give way to sleep, but this time exhausted after a day of traveling sleep came instantly.

It must have been about half past four in the morning when M woke up sweating. Sitting up straight in bed to recover from what appeared to be a nightmare, he reached for his mobile phone and sent a message.

The next morning, after having some fruit for breakfast, M went to the hotel lobby where a conference host was waiting. She took M to a speakers room near the backstage area, apparently avoiding the crowded conference reception center.

'Please, make yourself comfortable, Sir! I'll make sure Zander will be with you soon.'

M studied the room and glanced through the conference flyer on the coffee table where he had parked his speech notes. Just then, a tall and athletic man entered the room.

'Great to see you back in Cape Town, M! Are you well this morning?'

'Great to see you too, Zander! I am perfectly fine!

'By the way, did you get my message?'

'You mean the one you sent early this morning?'

'That's right!'

'I took care of it! By the way, put this vest on, just in case!'

'I guess, I've got about half hour left before I give my speech, right?'

'That's about right. I'll open the conference and then announce you as our main speaker. This will take about twenty minutes.'

Zander looked at his watch.

'I'll have to rush, I'm afraid.'

'Go right ahead, Zander! Ignore me!

'On the other hand, I'll join you. I need to go there anyway.'

The two men walked in the direction of the back stage area where they were stopped by a sturdy security guard. Perfectly instructed, the guard stepped aside when he recognized Zander and M. As the two men went backstage, M realized he had forgotten his notes.

'Zander, how ignorant of me to forget my speech notes. Let me fetch them quickly. I'll be back in a minute! You go ahead!'

'Will you please accompany our main speaker, Sir?' Zander asked the security guard.

The security guard followed M back to the speakers room, his hand on his gun. In a matter of minutes, they were back, M holding his speech notes. The guard attentively took M to a spot backstage where he could watch Zander give his introduction speech and then returned to his post.

M's mind wandered off as it often did just before a speech. Several minutes went by when the curtain near him began moving as if a breeze had ruffled its drapes. Strangely enough, M did not feel a draft. Then, a female hand appeared followed by its owner. For a minute, the woman stared M in the eye, her right hand behind her back.

'Hi!' she said.

'Nobody supposed to be backstage,' M thought.

He realized that Zander and the guard could not see the woman because the curtains blocked the view in both directions. Then, he remembered who this woman was.

'Abigail! It sure has been a very long time!'

'I am here to warn you!'

'Is this your destiny, Abigail?'

Her laugh sounded forced.

'How dare you talk to me like that!'

'Why is that Abigail?'

'As the Lord warned us, do not trust those who deny him.'

'Abigail, Abigail! You know better than that!'

'My belief is stronger than your words!'

'I am not questioning your belief, Abigail.'

'I wouldn't let you!'

'Now, what?' he asked.

'I cannot let you open this conference!'

'How will you stop me?'

'You'll find out!'

'Why, Abigail? Why?'

'I want the audience to see that you are but a prisoner when you crawl back into the cave, bleeding.'

'By turning me into a martyr, you'll achieve the opposite, Abigail! You'll create an event that might again be referred to for centuries.'

Not wanting to risk her opportunity, Abigail moved a few steps backwards and brought her right hand forward. A handgun was now pointing at M's chest.

Distracted by the voices in her mind, she failed to hear when Zander had finished his speech.

Suddenly, all lights were switched off as part of a surprise ceremony. After a few seconds, an orchestra started playing in crescendo and predawn-blue stage lights were switched on one by one.

M was no longer standing in front of her. Without looking, she pointed her handgun in the direction of the speaker pedestal and pulled the trigger. The noise of the gunshot was awful and her hand was jerked up by the force of the gunshot.

When she looked in the direction where Zander had been there was no pedestal to be seen. She heard the guard call for help and realized she'd missed her only chance. She brought the gun to her head, her finger slowly pulling the trigger, and closed her eyes.

Just before the trigger released the firing lever, the gun was ripped from her hand and she was thrown down to the ground. Held forcibly, she heard M address a baffled audience.

'Let me begin with two observations that have been inspired by the events that had just unfolded.

'First, many years ago, I met a person that I knew then would be a protector. Today, I had learned that my foresight was right.

'Second, no matter what happens, we should respect the aberrations of Nature, including ourselves, because like all that we observe, we are but the messengers of the conditions on our paths of history.'

At this point, Abigail, nearly unconscious, relaxed and surrendered. Zander tenderly lifted her from the stage floor and brought her to the ambulance which the guard had called for the moment he heard a shot.

That evening Phil had organized a reunion dinner for the group at OYO within walking distance of the conference hotel. When the group was seated, it soon became clear that everyone had heard his version of the story.

'How is she, Zander, and what happened?' Eve asked.

'She is stable now, although still in a state of shock. At the hospital, we learned that Abigail has a history of schizophrenia which started at about the time of our dialogue. Unfortunately she never received the care she needed. I made sure that would change.

'As for what happened, that's a bit of a story. Briefly, M sent me an urgent email message at five this morning about a dream in which "he was killed by someone familiar just before he was due to give his speech." He asked me to take the necessary measures, just in case.'

'So, what did you do?'

'To start with, I arranged for an armed guard and told him that nobody should be allowed to enter the backstage area. I also asked the security firm to bring a bulletproof vest to fit underneath a man's shirt. In hindsight, the most effective "measure" that I took was to bring in an element of surprise. I arranged for the dawn of an era to be simulated on stage following my introductory speech. During the few seconds that the lights were switched off, M went to a more theatrical stage spot and the speaker pedestal was mechanically lowered below the stage floor. This change of target location no doubt confused Abigail and gave us time to react. On the whole, we have been lucky. It could have been a lot worse if we had faced a professional!'

'You said that the guard would prevent anyone from entering the backstage area. So how did Abigail get there?' Phil asked.

'Well, M forgot his speech notes in the speakers room. I asked the guard to accompany him, just to be on the safe side. She must have entered during the few minutes that the guard left his post!'

Everyone in the group looked at M.

'I am philosophical about what has happened. We know that Nature keeps less optimal behavior patterns in the loop at times because they may contribute to the emergence of least-energy fitting patterns in the future.'

The Noordhoek Stroll Diagram

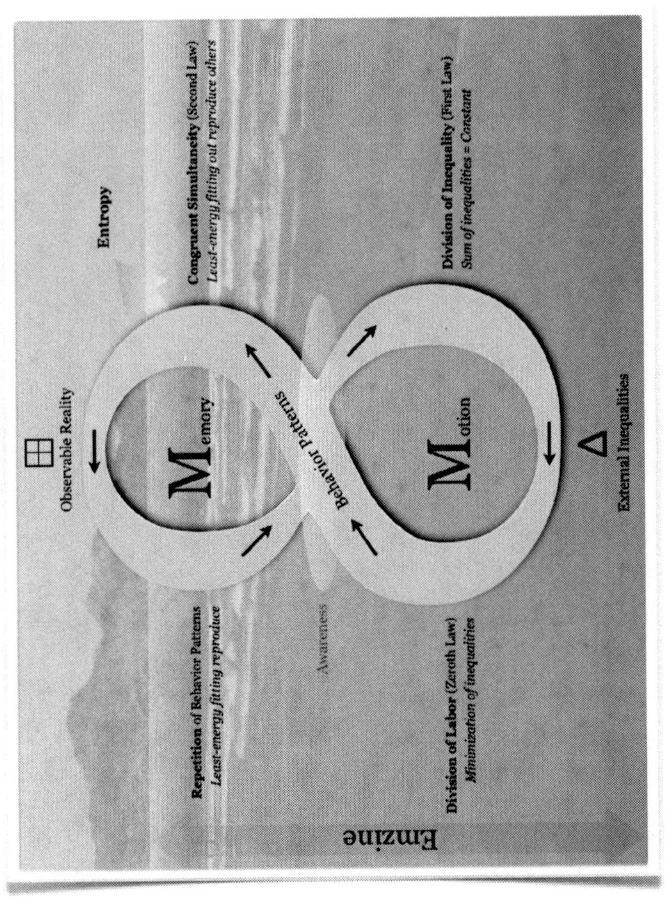

205

Call for Critique

To some, the dialogue in this book is controversial because it pulls the rug from underneath the established world views held in present-day science and religion. However, as the serious reader will agree, the intention of this book is not to shock but to offer new ways of looking at our world, ways that may help us improve our role in running it. Ideally, the ideas in this book will inspire academic research. You can share your comments or critique here: *http://www.emzine.net*

MAIN ASSERTION

Our world is a behavioral phenomenon where physical appearance is but a byproduct of reproducing behavior patterns.

THE DIVINE DOMAIN

We create meaning in our world through time. Yet, caught in a web of historical analyses, we run into a wall of timelessness or simultaneity.

REALITY'S AMAZING PARALLEL

Regardless of whether we observe natural or social phenomena, reality is but a reflection of a parallel world of simultaneity where behavior patterns emerge in distinct stages of development.

THE EMZINE PHENOMENON

Energy- and chaos-related matters are at heart of the emergence of behavior patterns. The realities in our mind emerge in the same way as the realities in our world, only the actors differ.

NO BEGINNING OR END
Motion and memory determine the way that Nature follows when generating the reality that we observe. The process of behavior-pattern emergence resonates with the fundamental laws of physics.

A NEW EXPERIENCE, A NEW SCIENCE
The parallel world of behavior-pattern development holds at every level and in every branch of the world that we observe.

TOWARD A MORE PREDICTABLE WORLD
The universal stages of emergence allow us to predict and improve the development of our world. Leaders are effective in specific stages of behavior-pattern development only.

FROM META-AWARENESS TO META-MORALITY
Notions of morality are bound to change from one stage of behavior-pattern emergence to another. A more participative relationship with Nature will eventually replace established theories about the divine.

ALCHEMIST NO MORE
We will become "creators."

THE PHILOSOPHERS' DREAM
The "behavioral" worldview presented in this book gives oxygen to the ideas of some important philosophers.

Acknowledgements

"Touched with fire," I wrote two books for different audiences in just a few years, both books hinting at a new explanation of our world.[16] Only then my ideas had matured enough to write *To Be Or To Become*, the apotheosis of my thinking. One would expect that after so much preparation I would no longer need much support. Nothing is less true.

I am very much indebted to Professor Hubert Kals who reviewed my manuscript as I progressed from chapter to chapter. He gave many a tactical hint. Most importantly, his growing enthusiasm stimulated the writing process. Hubert Kals inspired the character, Umberto.

I am also very much indebted to Jack Hydes, the author of a much used schoolbook on English poetry, for helping me ensure that my English language standards did not slip.[17]

I dedicate this book to my wife, Karen Evelien, as ever grateful for her unconditional support. She inspired the character, Eve.

---

[16] *A New Dimension of Time*, 2007 and *A New Leadership Ethos*, 2009

[17] *Touched with Fire*, Cambridge University Press, 1985

About the Author

Passionate speaker, leadership advisor, third-millennium philosopher, Marc van der Erve is regularly invited to address audiences on questions ranging from metaphysics to organization and leadership. He typically explores the practical and the philosophical on the crossroads where the natural and social sciences meet. Living abroad since many years, he was born and educated in The Netherlands. He holds a BSc in Applied Physics cum laude and a PhD in Sociology from Tilburg University. He resides in both South Africa and Europe.